LOW CHOLESTEROL
RECIPES FOR LIFE

CONTENTS

EDITORIAL
Managing Editor Catherine Saxelby
Food Editor Sheryle Eastwood
Assistant Food Editor Rachel Blackmore
Food Consultant Frances Naldrett
Editorial Co-ordinator Margaret Kelly
Editors Marian Broderick, Ingaret Ward
Home Economist Anneka Mitchell

PHOTOGRAPHY AND STYLING
Ashley Mackevicius
Rosemary De Santis

ILLUSTRATIONS
Carol Dunn

DESIGN AND PRODUCTION
Tracey Burt
Chris Hatcher

PUBLISHER
Philippa Sandall

Family Circle is a registered trademark of IPC Magazines Ltd
Published by J.B. Fairfax Press Pty Ltd by arrangement with IPC Magazines Ltd
© J.B.Fairfax Press Pty Ltd, 1990
Low Cholesterol Recipes for Life
Includes Index
ISBN 1 86343 012 1

Formatted by J.B. Fairfax Press Pty Ltd
Output by Savage Type, Brisbane
Printed by Toppan Printing Co. Hong Kong

Distributed by J.B. Fairfax Ltd
9 Trinity Centre, Park Farm Estate
Wellingborough, Northants
Ph: (0933) 402330 Fax: (0933) 402234

NUTRITION AND DIET GUIDE

EASY A TO Z LOW CHOLESTEROL RECIPES

METRIC MEASURES		QUICK METRIC IMPERIAL CONVERTER			
Cups					
¼ cup	60 mL				
⅓ cup	80 mL	**g**	**oz**	**mL**	**fl.oz**
½ cup	125 mL				
1 cup	250 mL	30	1	30	1
Spoons		60	2	60	2
¼ teaspoon	1.25 mL	125	4	125	4
½ teaspoon	2.5 mL	250	8	125	8
1 teaspoon	5 mL	370	12	370	12
1 tablespoon	20 mL	500	16	500	16

FOREWORD

Your heart is your body's most important organ. Each day, it pumps litres of blood to every organ, muscle and limb of your body. It, and its network of fine interconnecting blood vessels, needs to be kept in good shape.

Coronary heart disease is our nation's number-one killer. It accounts for one-third of all deaths each year, more than those from cancer and road accidents combined.

Yet it is a disease that is largely preventable. A healthy lifestyle is the best approach and this encompasses a sensible low fat daily diet, regular exercise, no cigarette smoking and stress control.

This book will set you on the path towards a healthier heart, whether you need to lower your blood cholesterol or are simply trying to prevent problems later in life. The recipes are low in saturated fats, low in cholesterol, low in salt and high in fibre. And there is sound information to help you understand more about cholesterol and what you can do to keep it low.

It will become your kitchen companion and make planning and preparing cholesterol-lowering meals much easier and more enjoyable.

CHECK-AND-GO

When planning a meal, use the easy Check-and-Go boxes which appear beside each ingredient. Simply check on your pantry shelf and if the ingredients are not there, tick the boxes as a reminder to add those items to your shopping list.

NUTRITIONAL ANALYSIS EXPLAINED

Each recipe has been computer-analysed for its kilojoule (calorie) content and food value. At a glance, you can see whether a dish is LOW, MEDIUM or HIGH in fat, cholesterol, sodium (a measure of salt) and fibre. The following recommended daily intakes have been used to set guidelines.

Kilojoules	8500
Calories	2000
Fat (based on 30% of kilojoules)	67 grams
Cholesterol	300 milligrams
Sodium	920 – 2300 milligrams
Fibre	25 – 30 grams

Note: A serve for dressings and sauces throughout this book is one tablespoon.

What is cholesterol?

Forget cholesterol, think fat!

Cholesterol is a white fat-like substance, which is produced by all animals, including humans. It is an essential component of the body, being vital for the manufacture of several hormones and vitamin D; the structure of cell membranes; and the formation of bile acids, which help digest fat.

✧ Cholesterol only becomes undesirable when large amounts accumulate in the bloodstream and cause fatty build-up in the blood vessels. Research shows that the higher your blood cholesterol reading, the higher the risk of heart problems – which can eventually lead to a heart attack or stroke.

✧ Heredity, being overweight, and doing too little exercise all influence blood cholesterol; but the major contributor is your diet, and in particular, the type and amount of fat you consume.

✧ Despite the recent emphasis on cholesterol in food, recent studies show that food fat, especially saturated fat, has a more direct influence on blood cholesterol than does food cholesterol.

✧ Eating large amounts of cholesterol (say from eggs or liver) does not automatically raise the blood cholesterol, as our liver

simply compensates by 'switching off' its own natural cholesterol manufacture.

✧ For saturated fats, there is no feedback mechanism and they actually encourage the liver to produce more cholesterol.

✧ For most people, cutting back on saturated fats is healthier than eliminating foods with high cholesterol, many of which are nutritious – such as eggs, organ meats and shellfish.

✧ A small number of people are sensitive to dietary cholesterol, and should avoid both fat and cholesterol.

SEPARATING FAT FROM FICTION

Reducing your overall fat intake has other benefits for health, and is an important nutrition goal in Western countries. Fat, whether saturated or unsaturated, is a concentrated source of kilojoules (calories) and provides twice as many kilojoules as either protein or carbohydrate, weight for weight.

✧ Apart from heart disease, high fat diets have also been linked to the development of other illnesses such as gallbladder disease and certain cancers.

FAT IN FOODS

Foods containing fat carry a mixture of saturated, polyunsaturated and monounsaturated fats.
The predominant fat gives the food its classification.

SATURATED	MONOUNSATURATED	POLYUNSATURATED
butter, cream, dripping, lard, copha	olive oil, olives	most vegetable oils, including safflower, sunflower, maize or corn, cotton seed, soya bean, grape seed, walnut, sesame
coconut oil, palm oil	peanut oil, peanuts, peanut butter	
many cheeses, ice cream, chocolate	most nuts	
meat fat, poultry skin	avocado	margarine, reduced-fat spreads and oils labelled polyunsaturated
full cream dairy products	egg yolk	seeds, including sunflower, pumpkin, sesame
many commercial foods including snack foods, pies, pastries, biscuits, fast foods, chips	margarine (unless labelled polyunsaturated)	nuts: walnuts, brazil nuts, pine nuts
	lean meat, chicken, salmon, tuna	fish, shellfish

7 Key steps for a healthy heart

How to lower your blood cholesterol

The latest medical research around the world points to these 7 key steps in lowering cholesterol and blood pressure and preventing fatal heart disease.

Reduce fats

1 Reduce your intake of all fats. Only 30 per cent of your total kilojoule (calorie) intake should come from fats, with saturated fats contributing no more than 10 per cent and unsaturated fats (poly- and monounsaturated) contributing the remaining 20 per cent.

Reduce weight

2 Reduce your body weight, if you are overweight.

Reduce cholesterol

3 Reduce cholesterol intake from foods to under 300 milligrams a day. This means limiting cholesterol-rich foods such as brains, liver, kidney, egg yolks, prawns, fish roe and squid.

Increase fibre intake

4 Increase your fibre intake. Water-soluble fibre, such as pectins and gums can speed the removal of cholesterol from the body. Pay attention to oats, oat bran, barley, barley bran, rice, rice bran, dried beans, lentils, fruit and vegetables.

Reduce salt

5 Reduce your salt intake. Do not sprinkle salt on food or in cooking, and switch to salt reduced or no-added-salt products when next shopping.

Reduce alcohol

6 Drink less alcohol. No more than two standard drinks a day is advisable.

Exercise more

7 Try to maintain a moderate level of exercise on a regular basis.

WATCH WHAT YOU EAT

	EAT AND ENJOY	EAT OCCASIONALLY	THESE FOODS ARE NOT FOR YOU
Grains and bread	oats, rice, buckwheat, barley, brans, wholegrain cereals, rolled oats (porridge), bran cereal, wheatgerm flour, bread, crispbread, pasta, noodles, macaroni, water crackers, filo pastry (with minimal oil)	modified cakes, biscuits and loaves made with ingredients in 'eat and enjoy' column	most toasted muesli, croissants, cheese, bread, commercial pastry, cakes, most biscuits and crackers
Vegetables and fruit	all fresh and frozen vegetables (canned vegetables preferably no added salt) dried peas, beans, and lentils canned beans (preferably no added salt) fresh fruit canned fruit (preferably unsweetened or in juice) dried fruit	olives, avocado pears	potato chips and other vegetables cooked in fat
Fish	all fresh fish canned fish (preferably no added salt) oysters, scallops, mussels, crab, lobster	prawns, fish roe, squid (calamari), cuttlefish, octopus – limit once per week	fried fish or shellfish in batter
Meat and poultry	lean beef, pork, veal, rabbit, game (venison, buffalo), lamb, mutton, chicken, turkey (skin removed), lean mince	liver, kidney, heart, sweetbreads – limit once per week lean ham, low fat luncheon meats (pressed turkey, chicken)	visible fat on meat (including poultry skin and pork crackling), sausages, salami, pate, luncheon meats (unless lean), bacon, brains
Nuts	chestnuts	walnuts, Brazil nuts, pecans, almonds, hazelnuts, peanuts, pine nuts, macadamias, pistachio, cashews all nuts (except chestnuts) are high in fat	coconut

	EAT AND ENJOY	EAT OCCASIONALLY	THESE FOODS ARE NOT FOR YOU
Fats and oils	all fats should be limited to 1 tablespoon per day	polyunsaturated oils monounsaturated oils polyunsaturated margarine low fat spreads	butter, lard, suet, dripping, ghee, copha, cooking margarine, solid frying fats, palm oil, palm kernel oil, coconut oil, hydrogenated vegetable oil whole or full cream milk
Fast foods and snacks	barbecued chicken (remove skin) toasted sandwiches, steak sandwiches, rolls, pocket flat bread with lean filling popcorn, rice crackers	hamburgers, pizzas	fried foods (chips, crumbed chicken, spring rolls, dim sims, battered fish, potato scallops) meat pies, sausage rolls, pasties, hot dogs fried rice, quiche potato crisps, corn chips (and similar snack foods)
Eggs	egg white yolk-free egg substitute	egg yolks – limit 2 per week	
Sweets and spreads		boiled sweets, fruit pastilles, chewing gum, peppermints jam, honey, marmalade, sugar peanut butter – limit 1–2 teaspoons a day	chocolate, caramels, toffee, butterscotch, muesli bars, lemon butter chocolate nut spread carob confectionery
Dairy foods	skim milk, low fat milk low fat yoghurt, frozen yoghurt low fat cheeses (cottage or curd cheese, quark, ricotta)	reduced fat cheeses, e.g.reduced fat Cheddar, feta, mozzarella, Swiss, Edam, ice confection	cream, sour cream, cream cheese hard yellow cheeses (unless reduced fat), cheese spreads, ice cream

Avocado

Avocados are often wrongly avoided by people with high cholesterol. Like other fruit and vegetables, they contain no cholesterol, but, at 20–25 per cent fat, they are high in fat, although their fat is mainly mono-unsaturated, a type not considered to raise blood cholesterol levels.

The high fat content of avocados makes them somewhat fattening and so they should be eaten sparingly by anyone with a weight problem.

Half an avocado supplies 1070 kilojoules (255 calories), which is equivalent to three or four slices of bread. So enjoy them with lemon juice, freshly ground pepper and crusty bread, but don't overindulge!

You might like to try this creamy sauce. Place an avocado, a banana, a little honey and fruit juice, in a food processor or blender and process to make sauce of pouring consistency. Serve this delicious sauce with fresh fruit salad in place of cream or ice cream. Avocado is also perfect sliced and tossed through a green salad.

Brans
(Except oat bran – see Oats)

Bran, in the form of unprocessed wheat bran, came to public prominence in the early 1970s, when British doctors believed the UK diet was severely lacking in food fibre. Since then, there has been a great deal of research into the nutritional attributes of the bran (outer layers) of many grains. Oat bran, rice bran, barley bran and maize (corn) bran can all be used as sources of fibre.

Most brans can be sprinkled over cereal, fruit or yoghurt, for a quick high fibre breakfast. They are also processed into packet breakfast cereals or incorporated into breads, pasta, biscuits, cakes, and even sausages, meat dishes and drinks.

Try our healthy bran recipes and see how easy it is to put more fibre into your food.

BRAN FIBRE

Wheat bran	40%
Oat bran	18%
Rice bran	26%
Barley bran	16%

Values are dietary fibre expressed as average values per 100 grams consumed.

GOLDEN-COATED CHICKEN DRUMSTICKS

Serves 4

- ☐ **4 x 150 g chicken drumsticks, skin removed**
- ☐ **plain flour**
- ☐ **1 egg, lightly beaten**
- ☐ **1 tablespoon polyunsaturated oil**

RICE BRAN COATING
- ☐ **¹/₂ cup (45 g) rice bran**
- ☐ **³/₄ cup (45 g) soft wholemeal bread crumbs**
- ☐ **¹/₄ teaspoon dried ground rosemary**
- ☐ **3 tablespoons grated Parmesan cheese**

1   To make coating, combine rice bran, breadcrumbs, rosemary and Parmesan cheese. Coat drumsticks with flour, dip in egg and coat well with crumb mixture.
2   Brush baking dish with oil. Add chicken and bake at 180°C for 1 hour, turning and basting frequently.

955 kilojoules (230 calories) per serve

Fat	*12.2 g*	*med*
Cholesterol	*131 mg*	*med*
Fibre	*3.0 g*	*high*
Sodium	*229 mg*	*med*

BRAN PASTRY

Makes 1 x 20 cm shell or 18 tartlets

- ☐ **1 cup (125 g) plain flour, sifted**
- ☐ **¹/₂ cup (45 g) rice bran**
- ☐ **2 tablespoons polyunsaturated oil**
- ☐ **¹/₂ cup (125 mL) skim milk**

1   Place flour and rice bran in a large mixing bowl.
2   Make a well in the centre and pour in oil and milk. Mix to a firm dough. Turn out onto a lightly floured board and knead lightly. Wrap in plastic food wrap. Refrigerate for 30 minutes. Roll out and line a pie plate. Bake at 200°C for 30–35 minutes.
To make a sweet pastry, add 2 tablespoons sugar and ¹/₂ teaspoon ground nutmeg.

Favourite Family Meatloaf, Golden-Coated Chicken Drumsticks

FAVOURITE FAMILY MEATLOAF

Serves 6

- ☐ **¹/₂ cup (60 g) bran cereal**
- ☐ **1 onion, grated**
- ☐ **1 carrot, grated**
- ☐ **1 small zucchini, grated**
- ☐ **3 tablespoons low fat unflavoured yoghurt**
- ☐ **1 egg, lightly beaten**
- ☐ **500 g lean minced beef**
- ☐ **2 teaspoons grated lemon rind**
- ☐ **1 tablespoon lemon juice**
- ☐ **¹/₂ teaspoon mixed dried herbs**
- ☐ **freshly ground black pepper**

TOPPING
- ☐ **4 tablespoons tomato sauce (no added salt)**
- ☐ **2 tablespoons Worcestershire sauce**
- ☐ **1 tablespoon white wine vinegar**
- ☐ **1 tablespoon red currant jelly**
- ☐ **3 tablespoons Mexican pumpkin seeds**
- ☐ **1 tablespoon toasted sesame seeds**

1   Combine bran cereal, onion, carrot, zucchini, yoghurt and egg in a mixing bowl. Set aside for 10 minutes.
2   Mix in meat, lemon rind, lemon juice, herbs and pepper to taste. Press mixture into a lightly greased and lined 25 cm x 10 cm ovenproof loaf pan. Bake at 180°C for 30–35 minutes. Drain off any excess liquid. Turn out onto an ovenproof plate.
3   To make topping, combine tomato sauce, Worcestershire sauce, vinegar and red currant jelly. Combine pumpkin and sesame seeds and sprinkle over top of meatloaf. Spread topping over all surfaces of meatloaf. Bake at 180°C for a further 10 minutes. Serve sliced either hot or cold.

842 kilojoules (202 calories) per serve

Fat	*9.1 g*	*med*
Cholesterol	*92 mg*	*med*
Fibre	*4.4 g*	*high*
Sodium	*169 mg*	*med*

MICROWAVE IT

Prepare the loaf mixture as above. Press it into a microwave-safe loaf dish. Cook on HIGH (100%) for 10–15 minutes. Turn out onto a microwave-safe plate and top with seed mixture. Spread loaf with topping and cook on HIGH (100%) for 4–5 minutes.

CHEESY SPINACH PIZZA

If you didn't think you could have pizza on a low cholesterol diet, you're in for a surprise. Try ours. It's low in fat and cholesterol and high in fibre.

Serves 8

☐ **8 spinach leaves, stalks removed and shredded**
☐ **¹/2 cup (20 g) unprocessed bran**
☐ **³/4 cup (190 mL) water**
☐ **2 tablespoons olive oil**
☐ **1 ³/4 cups (215 g) self-raising flour**
☐ **pinch ground nutmeg**
☐ **freshly ground black pepper**

TOPPING
☐ **4 tablespoons tomato paste (no added salt)**
☐ **1 tablespoon finely chopped fresh basil**
☐ **100 g mozzarella cheese, grated**
☐ **4 shallots, finely chopped**
☐ **2 tomatoes, sliced**
☐ **3 tablespoons grated Parmesan cheese**

1   Steam or microwave spinach until tender. Drain and set aside to cool.
2   Place bran and water in a mixing bowl. Stand 10 minutes, then stir in oil, flour, nutmeg, pepper to taste and one third of the cooked spinach.
3   Turn mixture out onto a lightly floured board and knead lightly. Press to fit a lightly greased 30 cm metal pizza tray.
4   To make topping, combine tomato paste with basil and spread over pizza base. Top with mozzarella, remaining spinach and shallots. Arrange tomato slices on top and sprinkle with Parmesan cheese. Bake at 200°C for 30–35 minutes or until golden.

881 kilojoules (210 calories) per serve

Fat	8.6 g	med
Cholesterol	12 mg	low
Fibre	3.6 g	high
Sodium	345 mg	high

Quick Banana Pecan Loaf, Cheesy Spinach Pizza

QUICK BANANA PECAN LOAF

A must for banana lovers. Serve this delicious quick bread as an alternative to bread or as a morning tea treat.

Serves 12

☐ **1 cup (45 g) unprocessed wheat bran**
☐ **1 cup (170 g) brown sugar**
☐ **3 small bananas, mashed**
☐ **1 cup (250 mL) skim milk**
☐ **60 g finely chopped pecans**
☐ **1 ¹/2 cups (185 g) self-raising flour, sifted**
☐ **1 teaspoon mixed spice**

1   Combine bran, sugar, bananas and milk in a mixing bowl. Set aside for 5 minutes.

2   Stir in pecans, flour and mixed spice. Spoon mixture into a lightly greased and lined 23 cm x 12 cm loaf pan. Bake at 200°C for 1 hour or until cooked.

770 kilojoules (182 calories) per serve

Fat	3.1 g	low
Cholesterol	0 mg	low
Fibre	3.0 g	high
Sodium	180 mg	med

NUTRITION TIPS

Because different brans have different actions in the body it is good to eat a variety of fibre foods.

❖ Wheat bran with its high content of insoluble fibre, is effective in providing bulk and relieving constipation.

❖ Oat and barley bran have a smaller effect on the bowel, but are useful for lowering blood cholesterol.

❖ Rice bran appears to lie between these, being good for laxation and heart health.

Breads

One of the oldest foods, bread, today comes in an amazing array of shapes, sizes and types. Wholemeal or wheatmeal bread is the most nutritious, offering the goodness of the whole grain with its abundance of fibre, B vitamins, essential minerals and proteins.

Mixed grain bread contains presoaked grains which add crunch and fibre but, because the basic dough is white, has a medium fibre content.

Bran-enriched bread contains wheat, oat or rice bran, and is valuable when a high fibre intake is important.

All types of bread, whatever their colour, are good for your heart, as they are low in fat and high in energy-giving complex carbohydrate. They are also not as fattening as we once believed. Often what is spread on top contributes more kilojoules (calories) than the bread underneath! So take care to spread butter or margarine sparingly and even avoid it entirely with high fat toppings like peanut butter, cheese, pate, and sardines. Bread contains no cholesterol and usually less than 3 percent fat.

BAKER'S TIP

Stale bread need not be wasted, it can be made into breadcrumbs. Trim the crusts from the bread and place on a baking tray, dry out in the oven at 150°C until bread is crisp and golden in colour. Place in a food processor and crumb. When cool, store in an airtight container.

❖

PUMPKIN AND PRUNE DAMPER

Serves 12

- [ ] 3 cups (375 g) self-raising flour, sifted
- [ ] 1 cup (135 g) wholemeal self-raising flour, sifted
- [ ] 2 teaspoons mixed spice
- [ ] 1/2 cup (20 g) unprocessed bran
- [ ] 3 tablespoons grape seed oil
- [ ] 1 egg, lightly beaten
- [ ] 300 g cooked mashed pumpkin
- [ ] 1 tablespoon grated orange rind
- [ ] 1/2 cup (90 g) chopped pitted prunes
- [ ] 1/2 cup (125 mL) orange juice
- [ ] 1/2 cup (125 mL) evaporated skim milk

1   Place both self-raising flours, mixed spice and bran in a bowl. Combine oil, egg, pumpkin, orange rind, prunes, orange juice and milk. Make a well in the centre of the dry ingredients and pour in pumpkin mixture. Mix lightly with a knife until all ingredients are just combined.
2   Turn mixture out onto a lightly floured board and knead lightly.
3   Place dough on a greased oven tray. Shape into a circle 2 cm thick. Brush with a little extra milk and mark into eight wedges with a sharp knife. Bake at 200°C for 45 minutes or until golden brown.

1066 kilojoules (252 calories) per serve

Fat	5.7 g	med
Cholesterol	20 mg	low
Fibre	4.9 g	high
Sodium	473 mg	high

Pumpkin and Prune Damper

HERB AND CHEESE LOAF

This high fibre loaf is terrific served warm.

Serves 12

- ☐ 1 ¹/₄ cups (170 g) self-raising wholemeal flour
- ☐ 1 cup (90 g) rolled oats
- ☐ 1 cup (45 g) unprocessed bran
- ☐ ¹/₂ cup (60 g) grated low fat cheese
- ☐ 1 tablespoon grated Parmesan cheese
- ☐ 2 tablespoons chopped chives
- ☐ 2 tablespoons chopped fresh parsley
- ☐ 1 cup (250 mL) low fat milk
- ☐ 4 tablespoons safflower oil
- ☐ 3 egg whites

1   In a bowl combine flour, rolled oats, bran, low fat and Parmesan cheeses, chives and parsley. Make a well in the centre of the dry ingredients. Add milk and oil. Mix to combine.
2   Beat egg whites until stiff peaks form. Lightly fold through dough.
3   Spoon into a 23 cm x 12 cm non-stick loaf pan. Bake at 180°C for 40 minutes.

678 kilojoules (161 calories) per serve

Fat	8.2 g	med
Cholesterol	7 mg	low
Fibre	3.6 g	high
Sodium	202 mg	med

CARROT AND SESAME MUFFINS

Delicious light muffins are perfect weekend fare. Any leftovers can be frozen and used when time is short.

Makes 24

- ☐ 3 cups (375 g) self-raising flour
- ☐ ¹/₂ teaspoon bicarbonate of soda
- ☐ 1 teaspoon mixed spice
- ☐ ¹/₂ cup (85 g) brown sugar
- ☐ 1 large carrot, grated
- ☐ 4 tablespoons toasted sesame seeds
- ☐ 1 cup (170 g) sultanas
- ☐ 1 cup (250 g) low fat unflavoured yoghurt
- ☐ 1 cup (250 mL) skim milk
- ☐ 3 tablespoons melted poly-unsaturated margarine (salt reduced)
- ☐ 3 egg whites, lightly beaten

1   Sift flour, bicarbonate of soda and mixed spice into a mixing bowl. Add brown sugar, carrot, sesame seeds and sultanas.
2   Combine yoghurt, milk, margarine and egg whites and stir into flour mixture. Mix until just combined. Spoon mixture into lightly greased muffin pans. Bake at 200°C for 20 minutes or until golden brown.

588 kilojoules (139 calories) per serve

Fat	3.6 g	low
Cholesterol	0 mg	low
Fibre	1.2 g	med
Sodium	214 mg	med

NUTRITION TIP

✧   For people who need to restrict salt as well as fat and cholesterol, try using a sodium-free baking powder in place of ordinary baking powder and self-raising flour, which supply a large amount of sodium. Based on potassium, it is available from pharmacies or specialty health food shops.
✧   Toasting bread does not reduce its carbohydrate or kilojoule (calorie) value. It merely drives off water and converts some of the starchy carbohydrate to dextrins and sugars.

Above: Herb and Cheese Loaf, Carrot and Sesame Muffins
Left: Fruit Cheese Dip, Ricotta Hearts

Cheese

Hard yellow cheeses have to be restricted or avoided on cholesterol-lowering diets, due to their high content of saturated fat, cholesterol and salt. Cheddar, one of the most popular varieties, averages 33% fat and is classified as high fat, together with Swiss, Parmesan, blue-vein, feta, Brie and cream cheese.

It is best to select low fat soft cheeses such as cottage cheese, ricotta and quark, or use small quantities of reduced fat versions of your favourite varieties. Many manufacturers now provide reduced fat Cheddar, Edam, Parmesan, mozzarella and other kinds.

❖

RICOTTA HEARTS

Serves 6

- ☐ **2 teaspoons gelatine dissolved in 1 tablespoon hot water**
- ☐ **250 g ricotta cheese,**
- ☐ **¹/2 cup (125 g) unflavoured low fat yoghurt**
- ☐ **2 tablespoons caster sugar**
- ☐ **1 egg white**
- ☐ **6 small strawberries, fanned**

STRAWBERRY COULIS
- ☐ **250 g strawberries, hulled**
- ☐ **1 tablespoon icing sugar**

KIWI COULIS
- ☐ **3 kiwi fruit, peeled and chopped**
- ☐ **1 tablespoon icing sugar**

1   Set gelatine mixture aside to cool. Rinse 6 heart shaped moulds in cold water and line with muslin.
2   Place ricotta, yoghurt, sugar and gelatine mixture in a bowl and mix well to combine.

3   Beat egg white until stiff peaks form and fold into cheese mixture. Fill moulds with cheese mixture. Place on a tray and leave to drain in the refrigerator overnight.
4   To make Strawberry Coulis, push strawberries through a sieve and mix in icing sugar. To make Kiwi Fruit Coulis, push kiwi fruit through a sieve and mix in icing sugar.
5   To serve, place a spoonful of each coulis on every plate and unmould the hearts in the centre. Garnish each heart with a fanned strawberry.

645 kilojoules (152 calories) per serve

Fat	4.0 g	low
Cholesterol	19 mg	low
Fibre	2.4 g	med
Sodium	111 mg	low

NUTRITION TIP

Low salt and reduced fat varieties of cheese are starting to appear in delicatessens and supermarkets. Salt is essential to cheese making, and cannot be completely eliminated, as it controls ripening and determines the final moisture content.

❖

FRUIT CHEESE DIP

Serves 6

- ☐ **¹/2 cup (60 g) dried apricots, finely chopped**
- ☐ **¹/2 cup (90 g) sultanas, finely chopped**
- ☐ **3 tablespoons glace ginger, finely chopped**
- ☐ **¹/2 cup (125 mL) brandy**
- ☐ **250 g low fat ricotta cheese**
- ☐ **125 g reduced fat cream cheese**
- ☐ **¹/2 teaspoon ground nutmeg**
- ☐ **2 teaspoons poppy seeds**

1   Place apricots, sultanas, ginger and brandy in a bowl, cover and soak overnight.
2   Place ricotta, cream cheese and nutmeg in a food processor or blender and process until combined. Drain fruit and mix into cheese mixture.
3   Chill until ready to serve. Sprinkle with poppy seeds and serve with melba toast or water crackers.

964 kilojoules (231 calories) per serve

Fat	10.7 g	med
Cholesterol	39 mg	low
Fibre	3.6 g	high
Sodium	180 mg	med

FILO CHICKEN PARCELS

For a wonderful luncheon, serve our tasty parcels with a green salad.

Serves 6

- ☐ **6 sheets filo pastry**
- ☐ **1 tablespoon olive oil**

FILLING
- ☐ **100 g broccoli, cut into small florets**
- ☐ **125 g cottage cheese**
- ☐ **1 tablespoon grated Parmesan cheese**
- ☐ **1 teaspoon Dijon mustard**
- ☐ **100 g cooked chicken, chopped**
- ☐ **freshly ground black pepper**

1 Brush each sheet of filo pastry with a little oil and fold in half.
2 Boil, steam or microwave broccoli until just tender. Drain and set aside.
3 Place cottage cheese, Parmesan cheese and mustard in a bowl and mix well to combine. Stir in broccoli and chicken. Season to taste with pepper. Place spoonfuls of mixture in the centre of each pastry sheet. Gather up the corners of the pastry over the filling to make a bag. Press together firmly and gently twist just above the filling to seal. Carefully fan out pastry tops and brush each parcel with remaining oil. Bake at 200°C for 20 minutes or until crisp and golden.

568 kilojoules (136 calories) per serve

Fat	5.4 g	med
Cholesterol	26 mg	low
Fibre	0.7 g	low
Sodium	163 mg	med

NUTRITION TIPS

✧ Cheese is a valuable source of calcium for strong bones and teeth, protein and riboflavin (vitamin B2). Because it is a concentrated form of milk, just 30 grams of cheese has the same food value as a 300 millilitre carton of milk. For people who do not consume milk or yoghurt, a small quantity of cheese each day is an important inclusion for calcium.

✧ Those who are unable to digest lactose (milk sugar) are usually able to eat firm varieties of cheese without ill effects. During cheesemaking, most of the lactose in milk is lost in the whey and any remaining is broken down as the cheese matures. Fresh unripened cheeses such as cottage cheese retain most of their lactose.

✧ Cheese makes a great snack. We have put together some cheesy snack ideas using low fat cheese which will allow you to indulge without worry.

✧ Season low fat cottage cheese with freshly ground black pepper and a few chopped fresh basil leaves. Place on a plain water cracker or crispbread and top with tomato and cucumber slices.

✧ Mix 2 tablespoons grated carrot, 1 tablespoon sultanas, 2 chopped dried apricots and a squeeze of lemon juice through 250 g ricotta cheese. Use as a topping on plain water crackers, crispbread or toast.

Filo Chicken Parcels, West Indian Chicken

KNOW YOUR CHEESES

LOW FAT	MEDIUM FAT	HIGH FAT
Cottage cheese	Edam	Cheddar
Creamed cottage cheese	Camembert	Gouda
Quark	Cheddar	Swiss
Ricotta (reduced fat)	Feta	Parmesan
	Mozzarella	Blue-vein
	Reduced-fat varieties of regular cheeses	Brie
		Stilton
		Gloucester
		Cream cheese
		Colby

Chicken

Chicken is a light and versatile white meat to include in a low fat, low cholesterol plan. Most of its fat lies just under the skin, which is easily removed for low fat cooking. The leanest cuts are breasts and breast fillets; the dark meat on thighs and drumsticks are higher in fat, although they can still be part of your diet. Sample our delicious recipes and discover how easy it is to prepare low fat fare.

❖

WEST INDIAN CHICKEN

Serves 4

☐ **750 g chicken pieces, skin removed**
☐ **1 teaspoon curry powder**
☐ **$^1/_4$ teaspoon ground ginger**
☐ **$^1/_4$ teaspoon ground cumin**
☐ **$^1/_4$ teaspoon ground cardamom**
☐ **pinch chilli powder**
☐ **$^1/_4$ teaspoon garam masala**
☐ **400 g canned pineapple pieces (no added sugar), drained and liquid reserved**
☐ **1 green capsicum, chopped**
☐ **freshly ground black pepper**

1   Score chicken pieces with a sharp knife. Combine curry powder, ginger, cumin, cardamom, chilli and garam masala and rub well into chicken pieces.
2   Place chicken in a shallow glass dish. Pour over reserved pineapple liquid and marinate for 2 hours. Remove chicken and grill slowly, turning and basting frequently with remaining pineapple liquid until tender.
3   Place pineapple pieces, any remaining liquid, capsicum and pepper to taste in a food processor or blender and process until smooth. Transfer to a saucepan and heat gently. To serve, place chicken on a serving platter and spoon over sauce.

856 kilojoules (206 calories) per serve

Fat	*5.3 g*	*med*
Cholesterol	*86 mg*	*med*
Fibre	*1.9 g*	*med*
Sodium	*95 mg*	*low*

❖

CHICKEN AND SPINACH PARCELS

If you are having a dinner party, these chicken parcels make a great main course. Prepare them earlier in the day and cook when required.

Serves 4

- ☐ **4 x 125 g boneless chicken fillets, skin removed**
- ☐ **4 tablespoons chicken stock**
- ☐ **4 tablespoons dry sherry**
- ☐ **freshly ground black pepper**

SPINACH FILLING
- ☐ **8 spinach leaves, stalks removed and leaves shredded**
- ☐ **1 large carrot, cut into thin strips**
- ☐ **1 stalk celery, cut into thin strips**
- ☐ **1 leek, cut into thin strips**
- ☐ **pinch ground nutmeg**
- ☐ **freshly ground black pepper**

1   Place chicken breasts between two sheets of plastic food wrap and pound lightly to flatten.
2   Steam or microwave spinach, carrot, celery and leek until tender. Refresh under cold running water. Pat dry on absorbent paper. Season to taste with nutmeg and pepper.
3   Cut four large squares of baking paper and top each with a chicken breast. Place spinach, carrot, celery and leek over half of each breast. Fold to enclose filling. Sprinkle with stock, sherry and pepper to taste. Seal the edges of the paper carefully and place on an oven tray. Bake at 200°C for 15–20 minutes or until tender. Season to taste with pepper. Chill for 1 hour before serving.

805 kilojoules (194 calories) per serve

Fat	5.5 g	med
Cholesterol	86 mg	med
Fibre	2.7 g	med
Sodium	126 mg	low

NUTRITION TIP

Like all meats, chicken provides valuable protein, B vitamins, and minerals such as iron and zinc. Its iron content is only about one-third that of red meat, but is nevertheless well absorbed by the body.

❖

ORIENTAL CHICKEN SALAD

Our light chicken salad is easy to prepare and makes a tasty alternative to heavier, more traditional chicken salads.

Serves 3

- ☐ **2 x 125 g boneless chicken fillets, skin removed**
- ☐ **1 large carrot**
- ☐ **¹/₂ bunch watercress**
- ☐ **¹/₄ red cabbage, shredded**
- ☐ **100 g bean sprouts**
- ☐ **4 tablespoons lime juice**

MARINADE
- ☐ **2 tablespoons dry sherry**
- ☐ **1 tablespoon low salt soy sauce**
- ☐ **2 teaspoons hoisin sauce**
- ☐ **2 teaspoons peanut oil**
- ☐ **2 cloves garlic, crushed**

1   Place chicken fillets between two sheets of plastic food wrap and pound lightly to flatten.
2   To make marinade, combine sherry, soy sauce, hoisin sauce, peanut oil and garlic in a glass bowl. Add chicken fillets and marinate for 1–2 hours.
3   Remove chicken from marinade and barbecue or grill slowly, turning and basting frequently with remaining marinade. Cool and slice thinly.
4   Using a vegetable peeler, slice carrot thinly lengthways. Stand slices in iced water for 5–10 minutes. Drain and arrange attractively on individual serving plates with watercress, cabbage and bean sprouts. Sprinkle with lime juice and top with chicken slices. Serve chilled.

1310 kilojoules (313 calories) per serve

Fat	6.9 g	med
Cholesterol	57 mg	med
Fibre	10.6 g	high
Sodium	320 mg	high

Dressings and Sauces

Dressings and sauces are frequently a health hazard for the heart, with their rich content of butter, cream, oil, eggs or cheese. Ours have been designed with a minimum of these ingredients and yet are delicious and convenient – they will add a new interest to salads, vegetables, fish, lean meats and pasta. A serve for dressings and sauces in this book is one tablespoon.

HOT CURRY SAUCE

As a topping for baked potatoes or an accompaniment to steamed vegetables this easy-to-prepare sauce makes a tasty change.

Makes 2 cups (500 mL)

- ☐ **6 zucchini, peeled and chopped**
- ☐ **2 teaspoons polyunsaturated oil**
- ☐ **1 onion, chopped**
- ☐ **1 teaspoon curry powder**
- ☐ **¹/₂ teaspoon chilli sauce**
- ☐ **1 tablespoon chutney or relish**

1   Boil, steam or microwave zucchini. Drain and set aside to cool.
2   Heat oil in a non-stick frypan. Add onion and curry powder and cook for 4–5 minutes or until onion softens.
3   Place zucchini, onion mixture, chilli sauce and chutney in a food processor or blender and process until smooth. Pour into a saucepan and cook over low heat until sauce heats through.

44 kilojoules (11 calories) per serve

Fat	0.4 g	low
Cholesterol	0 mg	low
Fibre	0.5 g	low
Sodium	4 mg	low

CHEESE SAUCE

Use this cheese sauce when making cauliflower cheese or lasagne.

Makes 1 cup (250 mL)

- ☐ **1 cup (250 mL) skim milk**
- ☐ **pinch ground nutmeg**
- ☐ **1 tablespoon cornflour blended with 2 tablespoons skim milk**
- ☐ **1 tablespoon grated Parmesan cheese**
- ☐ **freshly ground black pepper**

1   Bring milk and nutmeg to boil. Whisk in cornflour mixture and simmer for 10 minutes, stirring constantly.
2   Stir in cheese and cook a further 2 minutes. Season to taste with pepper.

61 kilojoules (14 calories) per serve

Fat	0.3 g	low
Cholesterol	0 mg	low
Fibre	0 g	low
Sodium	23 mg	low

MICROWAVE IT

To make Cheese Sauce, place milk and nutmeg in a microwave-safe jug, whisk in cornflour mixture. Cook on HIGH (100%) for 2 minutes or until sauce thickens. Stir in cheese and season to taste with pepper.

FRESH TOMATO AND BASIL SAUCE

Fresh tomato sauces are great with vegetables, chicken, fish or lean meats.

Makes 2 cups (500 mL)

- ☐ **1 tablespoon olive oil**
- ☐ **1 large onion, sliced**
- ☐ **1 clove garlic, crushed**
- ☐ **6 large tomatoes, peeled and diced**
- ☐ **¹/₂ cup (125 mL) tomato juice (no added salt)**
- ☐ **2 tablespoons chopped fresh basil**
- ☐ **freshly ground black pepper**

1   Heat oil in a saucepan. Cook onion and garlic for 4–5 minutes or until onion softens. Stir in tomatoes and tomato juice and simmer for 5 minutes.
2   Add 1 tablespoon basil and simmer for a further 1 hour or until sauce thickens and reduces. Just before serving, stir in remaining basil and season with pepper.

84 kilojoules (20 calories) per serve

Fat	0.7 g	low
Cholesterol	0 mg	low
Fibre	1.3 g	low
Sodium	22 mg	low

From left: Fresh Tomato and Basil Sauce, Cheese Sauce, Hot Curry Sauce

APPLE AND HERB DRESSING

Use this dressing as an alternative to the traditional French dressing or try it as a tasty dressing for rice salad.

Makes 1 $^1/_2$ cups (375 mL)

- ☐ **1 cup (250 mL) unsweetened apple juice**
- ☐ **3 tablespoons apple cider vinegar**
- ☐ **1 clove garlic, crushed**
- ☐ **1 tablespoon finely chopped chives**
- ☐ **2 tablespoons finely chopped fresh parsley**
- ☐ **freshly ground black pepper**

Place apple juice, vinegar, garlic, chives and parsley in a screwtop jar. Season to taste with pepper. Shake well to combine.

20 kilojoules (5 calories) per serve

Fat	0 g	low
Cholesterol	0 mg	low
Fibre	0.1 g	low
Sodium	2 mg	low

NUTRITION TIP

✧ When using commercial sauces, look for the many new 'no-oil' and 'fat-reduced' products now available.

✧ Check ingredients on the label; many mayonnaises are labelled 'poly-unsaturated' or 'egg-free', but are nevertheless high in fat.

MINTY LEMON DRESSING

Makes 1 cup (250 mL)

- ☐ **$^3/_4$ cup (190 mL) unflavoured low fat yoghurt**
- ☐ **1 clove garlic, crushed**
- ☐ **2 tablespoons lemon juice**
- ☐ **2 tablespoons chopped fresh mint**
- ☐ **freshly ground black pepper**

Combine yoghurt, garlic, lemon juice, mint and pepper in a bowl. Whisk to combine.

37 kilojoules (9 calories) per serve

Fat	0.2 g	low
Cholesterol	0 mg	low
Fibre	0.1 g	low
Sodium	13 mg	low

MOCK SOUR CREAM

One of the first foods to go when you start thinking about lowering your cholesterol intake is sour cream. Use our Mock Sour Cream in its place as a topping on potatoes, in soups or blended into casseroles.

Makes $^3/_4$ cup (190 mL)

- ☐ **3 tablespoons low fat milk**
- ☐ **1 teaspoon skim milk powder**
- ☐ **$^3/_4$ cup (190 g) low fat cottage cheese**
- ☐ **2 teaspoons white vinegar**

1 Whisk together low fat milk and skim milk powder

2 Combine half the milk mixture with half the cheese in a blender and blend until smooth. Add remaining milk mixture and cheese and continue to blend until a smooth mixture resembling sour cream is formed. Mix in vinegar.

94 kilojoules (23 calories) per serve

Fat	0.3 g	low
Cholesterol	3 mg	low
Fibre	0 g	low
Sodium	32 mg	low

COOK'S TIP

If kept in an airtight container in the refrigerator, Mock Sour Cream will keep for two to three days. You may add a little more vinegar if you prefer a more sour taste.

ITALIAN DRESSING

This tasty dressing can be prepared in advance and kept in the refrigerator to use as required.

Makes 1 cup (250 mL)

- ☐ ³/₄ cup (190 mL) red wine vinegar
- ☐ 2 tablespoons olive oil
- ☐ 1 clove garlic, crushed
- ☐ 2 teaspoons chopped fresh oregano
- ☐ 1 teaspoons chopped fresh basil
- ☐ freshly ground black pepper

In a screwtop jar combine vinegar, oil, garlic, oregano and basil. Shake to combine. Season to taste with pepper.

100 kilojoules (24 calories) per serve

Fat	2.7 g	low
Cholesterol	0 mg	low
Fibre	0.1 g	low
Sodium	0 mg	low

❖

TOFU MAYONNAISE

This delicious mayonnaise made with tofu is a cholesterol free alternative.

Makes 1¹/₂ cups (375 mL)

- ☐ 250 g tofu
- ☐ 1 teaspoon Dijon-style mustard
- ☐ 3 tablespoons cider vinegar
- ☐ ¹/₂ cup (125 mL) olive oil
- ☐ freshly ground black pepper

1   Place tofu, mustard and 1 tablespoon vinegar in a food processor or blender and process until smooth.
2 With the machine running, slowly add 2 tablespoons oil then 1 tablespoon vinegar. Continue in this way until all the oil and vinegar is used. Season to taste with pepper.

243 kilojoules (67 calories) per serve

Fat	7.1 g	med
Cholesterol	0 mg	low
Fibre	0 g	low
Sodium	0 mg	low

From left: Minty Lemon Dressing, Apple and Herb Dressing, Italian Dressing, Tofu Mayonnaise, Mock Sour Cream

Eggs

Eggs are limited to two per week, because of their high cholesterol content. At around 250 milligrams, just one egg brings you close to the recommended maximum of 300 milligrams a day. Virtually all the cholesterol and fat lies in the yolk; the white can be used freely, as can yolk-free substitute mixes.

Remember that the number of eggs eaten must be assessed in terms of your overall diet and blood cholesterol reading. If your intake of fats is low, and your blood cholesterol level within limits, then you could well enjoy more eggs more often. Check with your doctor or dietitian first.

Egg substitute is made from egg whites, skim milk powder, polyunsaturated vegetable oil, emulsifier and beta-carotene (the yellow-orange colour of carrots and many other vegetables). Its cholesterol is only a fraction that of eggs, and its fat is high in polyunsaturates. Although it cannot create a whole poached or boiled egg, it can be used to make omelettes, scrambled eggs, pancakes and in general cooking.

Polyunsaturated eggs contain a greater proportion of poly-unsaturated fat, but their cholesterol count is similar to ordinary eggs. The chickens are reared on a special feed rich in polyunsaturated seeds, blended from soyameal, sunflower seeds and grains, which alters the composition of the eggs they lay.

FAT FIGHTER

Flavoured vinegars are a boon as they add taste and interest without kilojoules (calories) or fat. Try making your own flavoured vinegars by steeping herbs, fruit or garlic in white or cider vinegar. Use flavoured vinegars in dressings, sauces and pickles that normally call for vinegar.

3 Key steps to eating for a healthy heart

Make your favourite recipes lighter and lower

Eating for a healthy heart doesn't mean giving up all your favourites. Cut back and keep the essential flavour with small changes to ingredients and cooking methods.

Reduce fats

1 Use as little oil, butter or margarine as possible when cooking. Cook in a non-stick pan or use a non-stick food spray. When stir-frying it is easy to cook 2 or 3 cups of chopped vegetables with just one tablespoon of oil in a preheated wok. Try lighter sauces or no-oil commerical salad dressings. Avoid snacks and keep to three meals a day. Biscuits, cakes, chocolates and packet snack foods are 'hidden' sources of fat (usually saturated).

Reduce salt intake

2 Gradually reduce the amount of salt you use in cooking and your taste buds will adapt after 2 to 3 weeks. Add extra flavour with double quantities of herbs and spices. Chilli, basil, garlic, coriander, rosemary and nutmeg are good choices for full flavour without salt. Beware salty sauces, they raise the salt content of your cooking (even if you're not actually adding salt) and should not be splashed on liberally. Shop for no-added-salt or salt reduced ingredients like canned tomatoes, cheese, margarine, sauce mixes, canned salmon and tuna.

Increase fibre

3 Switch to less refined foods such as brown rice, wholemeal bread and wholegrain or bran cereals rather than the more refined ones. Do not peel vegetables and fruit unless really necessary, instead just scrub them with a vegetable brush. Increase the serve size of vegetables, salads, grains and pasta on your plate and give more modest serves of meat. Create your own fresh fruit desserts in place of the sweet treats you're now indulging in.

STOCK TAKING

Homemade stocks are easy to make and contain none of the preservatives and salt of commercially prepared products.

CHICKEN STOCK

To make 2 litres of chicken stock you will require the carcass of one chicken, with all visible fat and any remaining skin removed. Place carcass in a large saucepan with 1 diced carrot, 6 stalks sliced celery, 2 large diced onions, herbs of your choice and $1/2$ teaspoon of peppercorns. Pour over 3 litres of water and bring to the boil, reduce heat and simmer for 2 hours, stirring occasionally. Strain stock and refrigerate overnight. Skim any fat from the surface and use as required.

VEGETABLE STOCK

To make 2 litres of vegetable stock you will require 1 head celery, 2 large onions, 2 carrots, a bunch of parsley and $1/2$ teaspoon peppercorns. Peel onions and chop. Wash and chop the celery, carrots and parsley, do not discard the celery leaves or the parsley stalks but keep them to use in the stock. Place all ingredients in a large saucepan with 2.5 litres of water. Bring to the boil, reduce heat and simmer for 30 minutes, stirring occasionally. Remove from heat and allow to cool. Puree the cold vegetable mixture, push through a sieve and use stock as required.

BEEF STOCK

Beef stock is made in much the same way as chicken stock but instead of using a chicken carcass use 500 g diced shin beef and 500 g marrow bones cut into pieces then make up as for chicken stock.

FREEZE IT

Make a quantity of stock and freeze it in $1/2$ cup (125 mL) or 1 cup (250 mL) portions, to use as required. It is also a good idea to freeze some in ice cube containers for those times when you may only require one or two tablespoons of stock.

Make your own stock for natural goodness and flavour

SIMPLE SUBSTITUTES
Low fat, low cholesterol

IF A RECIPE CALLS FOR:	USE:
Sour cream	Unflavoured non fat yoghurt, buttermilk, or soft tofu
Cream	Soft tofu, unflavoured non fat yoghurt, or canned evaporated skim milk
Cream cheese	Ricotta cheese blended with vanilla essence, a little caster sugar and grated lemon rind
Melted cheese on top	Half grated cheese, half breadcrumbs, half grated cheese, half crushed cornflakes or a fine sprinkle of sesame seeds
Butter	Polyunsaturated margarine, low fat spread or half butter, half oil
Coconut milk, coconut cream	One tablespoon desiccated coconut plus evaporated skim milk or unflavoured non fat yoghurt
Bacon	Lean ham
Shortcrust or puff pastry	Filo pastry or make a one crust pie

Essential Essences

Most desserts and sweets are loaded with fat and sugar. These are not only a danger to your heart, but also to your waistline and teeth, especially chewy sweet foods that cling around teeth for hours after eating. Here we present a selection of lighter, healthier alternatives, that we've flavoured with essences. They create a luscious flavour and aroma, needing only a touch of sugar or honey to taste perfect.

❖

APRICOT ALMOND DELIGHT

The delicate flavour and interesting texture of juicy apricots and toasted almonds complement each other beautifully in this light and fluffy dessert – perfect after any main course.

Serves 4

- ☐ **250 g dried apricots**
- ☐ **1 tablespoon gelatine, dissolved in 4 tablespoons hot water**
- ☐ **1 cup (250 mL) evaporated skim milk**
- ☐ **3 tablespoons caster sugar**
- ☐ **1 teaspoon almond essence**
- ☐ **1 tablespoon finely chopped toasted almonds**

1   Place apricots in a bowl, pour in sufficient water to cover and leave to soak overnight.
2   Drain apricots and place in a food processor or blender with gelatine mixture, skim milk, sugar and almond essence. Process until smooth. Pour into individual glasses. Refrigerate until firm. To serve sprinkle with almonds.

1105 kilojoules (260 calories) per serve

Fat	1.4 g	low
Cholesterol	2 mg	low
Fibre	18 g	high
Sodium	109 mg	low

❖

COFFEE MERINGUES

Who would believe that these delicious morsels are free of fat and cholesterol? They are perfect to serve with coffee or as an afternoon tea treat.

Makes 30

- ☐ **³/₄ cup (185 g) raw sugar**
- ☐ **3 tablespoons water**
- ☐ **1 egg white**
- ☐ **1 teaspoon white vinegar**
- ☐ **2 teaspoons cornflour**
- ☐ **2 teaspoons coffee essence**

1   Place sugar and water in a small saucepan, over a medium heat, stirring until sugar dissolves. Bring to the boil and boil for 1–2 minutes. Brush any sugar grains from sides of pan with a wet pastry brush.
2   Beat egg white until stiff peaks form. Continue beating while pouring in hot syrup in a thin stream, a little at a time. Beat until meringue is thick. Fold in vinegar, cornflour and coffee essence.
3   Place mixture in a large piping bag fitted with a fluted tube. Pipe 4 cm stars onto greased and lined oven trays. Bake at 140°C for 1 hour or until firm and dry. Cool in oven with door ajar.

162 kilojoules (38 calories) per serve

Fat	0 g	low
Cholesterol	0 mg	low
Fibre	0 g	low
Sodium	3 mg	low

❖

STRAWBERRY AND RICE CREAM

A creamy fruit dessert that will be a hit with all the family. For something different you might like to try apricots with almond essence.

Serves 4

- ☐ **¹/₂ cup (100 g) short grain rice**
- ☐ **200 g fresh strawberries, hulled and halved**
- ☐ **¹/₂ cup (125 mL) low fat unflavoured yoghurt**
- ☐ **³/₄ cup (190 mL) evaporated skim milk**
- ☐ **1 tablespoon caster sugar**
- ☐ **¹/₂ teaspoon strawberry essence**

1   Cook rice in a saucepan of boiling water for 10–12 minutes or until just tender. Drain and rinse under cold running water.
2   Combine rice, strawberries, yoghurt, milk, sugar and essence. Spoon rice cream into four individual dishes. Refrigerate until well chilled.

631 kilojoules (150 calories) per serve

Fat	3.0 g	low
Cholesterol	4 mg	low
Fibre	1.9 g	med
Sodium	114 mg	low

THE ESSENCE

✧ Essences can be produced in one of three ways: by steeping the ingredient in water or alcohol; by distillation; or by synthetic chemical compounds. By far the best are those made naturally, the flavour is truer and while you will find them a little more expensive the end result is well worth it.

✧ Essences should be purchased in small quantities and are best if used within three months.

✧ Always store essences in tightly stoppered bottles in a cool, dark place, this will ensure that the maximum flavour is retained.

✧ It is believed that rosewater – one of the sweet smelling essences – was originally brought to India by the Moguls. It became a fashionable flavouring in England during the 16th Century and remained a staple ingredient until Victorian times.

✧ One of the first uses for rosewater in the Western world was to scent the finger bowls of the wealthy.

✧ As the name implies rosewater is extracted from roses.

✧ Rosewater and orange flower water are essential ingredients in Indian and Middle Eastern cooking, where they are used in both savoury and sweet dishes.

✧ Other popular essences include peppermint, almond and vanilla.

Apricot Almond Delight, Coffee Meringues, Strawberry and Rice Cream

Fish

Fish – light, appetising and nutritious – plays a key role in lowering your cholesterol. It is low in fat and cholesterol, it helps with weight control, being so low in kilojoules (calories), and it is rich in omega-3 fats, which are now believed to protect the heart against disease.

Omega-3 fats reduce the tendency for the blood to clot and so lessen its 'stickiness'. They can lower blood pressure and reduce the fatty build up on blood vessel walls. They occur in all fish but are particularly rich in oily fish like herring, salmon, tuna, mackerel, sardines and ocean trout. Aim to eat fish at least three times a week, including fresh, frozen and canned for variety. Follow the ideas in our recipes for new and interesting ways to prepare fish.

FAT FIGHTERS

Forget frying fish in fat. Instead, try one of the many methods of cooking fish without fat.

◇ Microwave in a little skim milk and chopped herbs. Cook 500 g fish fillets covered on HIGH (100%) for 4–5 minutes.

◇ Poach in a flavoursome stock.

◇ 'Dry fry' in a pan that has been sprayed with non-stick spray or lined with a silicon-coated paper liner.

◇ Barbecue whole fish wrapped in foil. Squeeze lemon juice into the cavity of the fish and fill with lemon slices and sprigs of dill or mint. Wrap in two layers of foil and cook on barbecue for 25–30 minutes, or until flesh flakes when tested with a fork.

Fish and Basil Vermicelli Soup,
Salmon Cutlets with Basil Sauce,
Thai Flavoured Whole Chilli Fish

THAI FLAVOURED WHOLE CHILLI FISH

For this delicious fish dish we used baby bream but you might like to use small snapper or similar small fish.

Serves 4

- ☐ **4 small whole fish**
- ☐ **1 red chilli, seeded and finely sliced**

MARINADE
- ☐ **1 tablespoon chopped fresh coriander (including root and stem)**
- ☐ **1 teaspoon grated fresh ginger**
- ☐ **1 clove garlic, crushed**
- ☐ **$1/2$ teaspoon chilli paste (sambal ulek)**
- ☐ **1 teaspoon sugar**
- ☐ **2 teaspoons ground turmeric**
- ☐ **1 tablespoon peanut oil**
- ☐ **1 tablespoon vinegar**
- ☐ **1 tablespoon water**

1   Clean fish and rinse under cold running water. Pat dry with absorbent kitchen paper and arrange in a deep tray.
2   To make marinade, combine coriander, ginger, garlic, chilli paste, sugar, turmeric, oil, vinegar and water. Pour over fish and rub well into the skin and flesh. Cover and refrigerate for 2 hours.
3   Barbecue or grill fish for 3–4 minutes each side or until flesh flakes when tested with a fork. Serve fish with any remaining marinade. Top with chilli slices.

945 kilojoules (224 calories) per serve

Fat	8.4 g	med
Cholesterol	120 mg	med
Fibre	0.3 g	low
Sodium	240 mg	med

❖

SALMON CUTLETS WITH BASIL SAUCE

Serves 4

- ☐ **4 x 125 g salmon cutlets**
- ☐ **freshly ground black pepper**

BASIL SAUCE
- ☐ **1 bunch fresh basil, leaves removed**
- ☐ **2 tablespoons lemon juice**
- ☐ **1 tablespoon olive oil**
- ☐ **1 clove garlic, crushed**
- ☐ **4 tablespoons grated Parmesan cheese**
- ☐ **3 tablespoons pine nuts, toasted**

1   Place fish cutlets in a glass dish and season with pepper to taste.
2   To make sauce, place basil leaves, lemon juice, olive oil, garlic, Parmesan and pine nuts in a food processor or blender and process until smooth.
3   Spoon half the basil sauce over fish. Cover and refrigerate for 30 minutes. Grill or barbecue fish for 4–5 minutes each side or until flesh flakes when tested with a fork. Serve fish with remaining sauce.

963 kilojoules (230 calories) per serve

Fat	14.2 g	high
Cholesterol	84 mg	med
Fibre	0.7 g	low
Sodium	274 mg	high

❖

FISH AND BASIL VERMICELLI SOUP

Serves 6

- ☐ **1 tablespoon olive oil**
- ☐ **1 onion, finely chopped**
- ☐ **2 cloves garlic, crushed**
- ☐ **800 g canned tomatoes (no added salt), undrained and mashed**
- ☐ **3 tablespoons tomato paste (no added salt)**
- ☐ **$1/2$ teaspoon sugar**
- ☐ **3 cups (750 mL) water**
- ☐ **1 kg fish cutlets, such as mackerel or groper**
- ☐ **2 teaspoons grated lemon rind**
- ☐ **2 tablespoons finely chopped fresh basil**
- ☐ **100 g vermicelli**
- ☐ **freshly ground black pepper**

1   Heat oil in a large saucepan. Cook onion and garlic for 2–3 minutes or until onion softens. Stir in tomatoes, tomato paste, sugar and 1 cup (250 mL) water. Bring to the boil, reduce heat and simmer covered for 10 minutes.
2   Poach fish cutlets in remaining 2 cups (500 mL) of water, drain and reserve cooking liquid. Remove skin from fish and flake into large pieces.
3   Add lemon rind, basil, vermicelli and reserved liquid. Cover and simmer for 5–6 minutes or until vermicelli is cooked. Season to taste with pepper. Stir in fish and cook 2–3 minutes to heat through.

938 kilojoules (183 calories) per serve

Fat	6.9 g	med
Cholesterol	100 mg	med
Fibre	1.8 g	med
Sodium	216 mg	med

MARINATED CITRUS FISH SALAD

Serves 4

- [ ] **500 g white fish fillets, cut into strips**
- [ ] **2 teaspoons pink peppercorns**
- [ ] **2 teaspoons orange rind**
- [ ] **400 g canned lychees, drained**
- [ ] **1 orange, peeled and segmented**
- [ ] **1 grapefruit, peeled and segmented**
- [ ] **¹/₂ bunch fresh watercress**

MARINADE
- [ ] **1 tablespoon grape seed oil**
- [ ] **¹/₂ cup (125 mL) orange juice**
- [ ] **1 tablespoon grapefruit juice**
- [ ] **1 tablespoon lime juice**
- [ ] **1 tablespoon tarragon vinegar**
- [ ] **1 teaspoon grated fresh ginger**

1   Place fish in a glass bowl with peppercorns and orange rind.
2   To make marinade, combine oil, orange, grapefruit and lime juices, vinegar and ginger. Pour marinade over fish, cover and refrigerate overnight.
3   To serve, remove fish with a slotted spoon to a bowl. Add lychees, orange and grapefruit segments to fish mixture. Toss lightly to combine. Arrange watercress on a plate and top with fish salad. Spoon over a little of the marinade.

1104 kilojoules (262 calories) per serve

Fat	*7.1 g*	*med*
Cholesterol	*75 mg*	*med*
Fibre	*3.4 g*	*high*
Sodium	*177 mg*	*med*

❖

TUNA PATE

Serves 4

- [ ] **200 g canned tuna in springwater, drained**
- [ ] **1 small Lebanese cucumber, peeled, seeded and chopped**
- [ ] **1 cup (250 mL) tomato juice (no added salt)**
- [ ] **1 ¹/₂ tablespoons gelatine dissolved in ¹/₂ cup (125 mL) hot water**
- [ ] **1 tablespoon chopped fresh dill**
- [ ] **1 teaspoon grated lemon rind**
- [ ] **1 teaspoon lemon juice**
- [ ] **2 teaspoons finely chopped capers**
- [ ] **1 teaspoon horseradish relish**
- [ ] **3 tablespoons low fat unflavoured yoghurt**
- [ ] **freshly ground black pepper**

1   Place tuna, cucumber, tomato juice, gelatine mixture, dill, lemon rind, lemon juice, capers, horseradish relish and yoghurt in a food processor or blender. Process until smooth.
2   Season to taste with pepper. Pour tuna mixture into four individual dishes. Refrigerate until firm.

371 kilojoules (88 calories) per serve

Fat	*5.8 g*	*low*
Cholesterol	*23 mg*	*low*
Fibre	*0.8 g*	*low*
Sodium	*108 mg*	*low*

SATAY SALMON PATTIES

Serves 6

- ☐ 440 g canned red salmon, no added salt, well drained and flaked
- ☐ 3 medium potatoes, cooked and mashed
- ☐ 2 tablespoons plain flour
- ☐ 1 clove garlic, crushed
- ☐ 1 teaspoon grated fresh ginger
- ☐ 1 teaspoon grated lemon rind
- ☐ 1 small red chilli, seeded and finely chopped
- ☐ 2 teaspoons low salt soy sauce
- ☐ 1 teaspoon curry paste (vindaloo)
- ☐ pinch of chilli powder
- ☐ $^1/_4$ teaspoon ground cumin
- ☐ 2 tablespoons finely chopped unsalted roasted peanuts
- ☐ $^1/_2$ cup (60 g) sesame seeds
- ☐ $^1/_2$ cup (60 g) dry breadcrumbs
- ☐ 1 tablespoon peanut oil

1   Combine salmon, potatoes, flour, garlic, ginger, lemon rind, chilli, soy sauce, curry paste, chilli powder, cumin and peanuts in a large mixing bowl.

2   Combine breadcrumbs and sesame seeds. Shape salmon mixture into twelve patties. Roll in sesame seed mixture and refrigerate for 30 minutes. Brush the base of a non-stick frypan with oil and heat. Cook patties for 3–4 minutes each side or until golden brown. Remove from pan and drain on absorbent kitchen paper.

1635 kilojoules (389 calories) per serve

Fat	*19.1 g*	*high*
Cholesterol	*66 mg*	*med*
Fibre	*2.1 g*	*med*
Sodium	*161 mg*	*med*

❖

FISH KEBABS WITH BANANA SAUCE

Serves 6

- ☐ 750 g white fish fillets, cut into 5 cm cubes
- ☐ 1 tablespoon peanut oil

BANANA SAUCE
- ☐ 20 g polyunsaturated margarine
- ☐ 3 tablespoons brown sugar
- ☐ $^3/_4$ cup (190 mL) evaporated skim milk
- ☐ $^3/_4$ cup (185 g) low fat unflavoured yoghurt
- ☐ 4 medium bananas, sliced
- ☐ 2 tablespoons chopped nuts, toasted

1   Thread fish onto twelve oiled wooden skewers. Brush with oil and grill or barbecue for 3–4 minutes each side.
2   To make sauce, melt margarine in a frypan. Remove pan from heat.
3   Dissolve brown sugar in evaporated milk. Stir evaporated milk mixture and yoghurt into melted margarine. Add bananas and nuts and cook gently over low heat for 1–2 minutes.
4   Arrange kebabs on a serving plate, spoon over sauce and serve immediately.

1523 kilojoules (362 calories) per serve

Fat	*12.3 g*	*med*
Cholesterol	*78 mg*	*med*
Fibre	*2.3 g*	*med*
Sodium	*256 mg*	*high*

Above: Satay Salmon Patties, Tuna Pate
Left: Marinated Citrus Fish Salad, Fish Kebabs with Banana Sauce

❖

FISH CUTLETS WITH ITALIAN SAUCE

Serves 4

- ☐ 4 x 150 g white fish cutlets
- ☐ 2 tablespoons lemon juice
- ☐ 6 shallots, finely chopped
- ☐ 1 clove garlic, crushed
- ☐ 400 g canned tomatoes (no added salt)
- ☐ 200 g button mushrooms, sliced
- ☐ $1/2$ cup (125 mL) red wine
- ☐ 2 teaspoons finely chopped fresh basil
- ☐ $1/2$ teaspoon dried oregano
- ☐ freshly ground black pepper
- ☐ 2 tablespoons grated Parmesan cheese

1 Brush fish cutlets with lemon juice. Place under a preheated griller and cook for 4–5 minutes each side. Remove from griller and keep warm.

2 Place shallots, garlic, tomatoes, mushrooms, wine, basil, oregano and pepper to taste in a saucepan. Bring to the boil. Reduce heat and simmer gently for 8–10 minutes.

3 Arrange fish cutlets on serving plates. Spoon sauce over and top with Parmesan cheese.

876 kilojoules (206 calories) per serve

Fat	*4.5 g*	*low*
Cholesterol	*92 mg*	*med*
Fibre	*1.8 g*	*med*
Sodium	*225 mg*	*med*

Left: Fish Cutlets with Italian Sauce
Right: Salmon Souffles

FISHY TALES

A guide to buying fresh fish

	LOOK FOR	WATCH OUT FOR
Fillets	Fillets should be shiny and firm with a pleasant sea smell	Fillets that are dull, soft, discoloured or 'ooze' water when touched indicate fish that is past its best.
Whole Fish	Whole fish should have a pleasant sea smell and a bright lustre to the skin. Gills should be red and the eyes bright and bulging. When touched, the flesh should be firm and springy.	Dull-coloured fish with sunken eyes should be avoided at all costs.

SALMON SOUFFLES

Serves 4

- ☐ **220 g canned red salmon, no added salt, drained and flaked**
- ☐ **100 g bottled oysters, drained, rinsed and chopped**
- ☐ **2 teaspoons finely chopped capers**
- ☐ **1 teaspoon finely chopped fresh dill**
- ☐ **2–3 dashes Tabasco sauce**
- ☐ **1 cup (250 g) low fat cottage cheese**
- ☐ **freshly ground black pepper**
- ☐ **4 egg whites**

1 Combine salmon, oysters, capers, dill, Tabasco and cottage cheese in a bowl. Season to taste with pepper.

2 Beat egg whites until stiff peaks form and fold lightly through salmon mixture. Spoon into four lightly greased individual souffle dishes and bake at 200°C for 30–35 minutes.

550 kilojoules (132 calories) per serve

Fat	2.2 g	low
Cholesterol	54 mg	med
Fibre	0.2 g	low
Sodium	385 mg	high

COOK'S TIP

When incorporating egg whites into a mixture, firstly mix in 1 tablespoon of the beaten egg whites, this loosens the mixture and makes it easier to fold in the remaining egg whites.

FINISHING TOUCHES

Fruit

Fresh fruit – juicy, sweet and luscious – is one of the nicest and healthiest ways to end a meal. With fruit, you can satisfy a sweet tooth, and keep your heart healthy too. And for day-to-day sweets, nothing can compare with a beautiful ripe peach, a crunchy apple or a juicy pear for nutrition, convenience and flavour.

Fruit is good for your heart because it has negligible amounts of fat and lots of fibre. Its fibre is rich in gums and pectins, which are known to lower blood cholesterol and slow the absorption of food. The fibre also creates 'bulk' and makes fruit a filling snack between meals.

Dried fruits are a useful addition to your diet. Sultanas, raisins, dried apricots, dates, prunes and figs, have a natural sweetness (being high in fruit sugars), no fat, and an excellent fibre content. Yoghurt and desserts are enlivened with a handful of dried fruit; meat and poultry team particularly well with apricots, currants and prunes; salads take on a new air with a touch of fruity sweetness.

We've devised a collection of fruity recipes to inspire and delight you and your family.

All recipes are sweetened subtly, with a little sugar or honey, sometimes with a dash of liqueur. This allows the fruit's delectable flavour to come through, enhanced with the help of spices or grated rinds.

Blueberry Mousse, Mango Raita, Hot Bananas and Oranges

BLUEBERRY MOUSSE

This pretty dessert is the perfect way to finish any dinner party. When fresh blueberries are in season they are the ideal garnish.

Serves 8

- ☐ **400 g canned blueberries, drained and liquid reserved**
- ☐ **3 tablespoons caster sugar**
- ☐ **2 tablespoons gelatine**
- ☐ **1 cup (250 mL) evaporated skim milk, chilled**
- ☐ **1 cup (250 g) low fat unflavoured yoghurt**

1　In a food processor or blender puree blueberries and sugar. Strain and discard skins. Dissolve gelatine in $^3/_4$ cup (185 mL) of warmed reserved blueberry liquid. Whip evaporated milk until thick and beat in yoghurt. Mix in gelatine mixture and fold through blueberry puree.

2　Spoon mousse into a wet mould, or eight individual moulds, cover and chill until set. Unmould and serve.

657 kilojoules (154 calories) per serve

Fat	0.5 g	low
Cholesterol	4 mg	low
Fibre	2.2 g	med
Sodium	116 mg	low

MANGO RAITA

Raitas are soothing yoghurt-based relishes. Traditionally served with curries, they act as a palate cooler. We have used mangoes and bananas in our raita, you might prefer to use only mangoes or bananas.

Serves 6

- ☐ **2 cups (500 g) low fat unflavoured yoghurt**
- ☐ **1 mango, diced**
- ☐ **1 banana, diced**
- ☐ **2 tablespoons finely chopped fresh mint**
- ☐ **$^1/_2$ teaspoon ground cumin**
- ☐ **pinch chilli powder**

Beat yoghurt until smooth. Fold in mango, banana, mint, cumin and chilli powder.

373 kilojoules (89 calories) per serve

Fat	1.0 g	low
Cholesterol	6 mg	low
Fibre	1.3 g	med
Sodium	68 mg	low

NUTRITION TIPS

Most fruit provide vitamins, but some stand head and shoulders above the rest. Citrus fruit, berries, guava, kiwi fruit and pawpaw are the fruit richest in vitamin C, and worth eating on a daily basis. Orange-coloured fruit like apricots, mangoes, and rockmelon are rich in beta-carotene (the precursor of vitamin A).

✧ If your children refuse to eat vegetables, remember that fruit is the ideal substitute. Fruit supplies the same nutrients as vegetables, notably vitamins A and C, fibre and essential minerals such as potassium. Most children will happily tuck into a piece of fruit or cut-up portions with no worries.

✧ Beware of too much fruit juice! Fruit juice is fruit in concentrated form, with its fibre removed. Drinking a glass of orange juice takes no effort. Eating your way through the equivalent of two or three oranges is much harder. The kilojoules (calories) are the same!

HOT BANANAS AND ORANGES

Barbecuing is the perfect way to cook this easy dessert. But it is just as good baked in the oven.

Serves 4

- ☐ **1 teaspoon polyunsaturated oil**
- ☐ **4 bananas, peeled and sliced in half lengthways**
- ☐ **4 tablespoons orange juice**
- ☐ **1 orange, segmented**
- ☐ **1 tablespoon brown sugar**

1　Cut four pieces of aluminium foil large enough to wrap around the bananas. Brush foil very lightly with polyunsaturated oil. Place two banana halves side by side on each piece of foil. Sprinkle 1 tablespoon orange juice over each banana. Divide orange segments and sugar into four portions and spoon over bananas.

2　Wrap foil around bananas and oranges to form a parcel. Cook on the barbecue for 15–20 minutes or in the oven at 180°C.

681 kilojoules (163 calories) per serve

Fat	1.2 g	low
Cholesterol	0 mg	low
Fibre	4.3 g	high
Sodium	3 mg	low

BERRY STRUDEL

For our strudel we use a little polyunsaturated oil instead of butter and in this way provide the perfect dessert for any cholesterol watcher.

Serves 8

- ☐ **6 sheets filo pastry**
- ☐ **1 tablespoon polyunsaturated oil**
- ☐ **2 tablespoons icing sugar, sifted**

FILLING

- ☐ **200 g fresh raspberries**
- ☐ **250 g fresh strawberries, halved**
- ☐ **1 tablespoon caster sugar**
- ☐ **3 tablespoons ground almonds**

1   Brush two sheets of pastry with oil and stack alternately with unoiled sheets.

2   Combine strawberries, raspberries and sugar, toss to combine.

3   Sprinkle pastry with almonds, top with berry mixture, leaving 2.5 cm around all edges. Fold in the long edges of the pastry. Starting from the short edge roll up the strudel. Place on an oven tray lined with baking paper. Bake at 200°C for 20–25 minutes or until golden. Just before serving sprinkle with icing sugar.

581 kilojoules (138 calories) per serve

Fat	6.1 g	med
Cholesterol	0 mg	low
Fibre	4.0 g	high
Sodium	77 mg	low

Berry Strudel, Watermelon and Strawberry Sorbet

❖

WATERMELON AND STRAWBERRY SORBET

Sorbets or water ices are light and refreshing. The perfect dessert to serve at a summer luncheon or as a palate cleanser during the meal. We have made our sorbet with watermelon and strawberries, you might like to try other favourite fruits.

Serves 8

- ☐ **1 cup (250 mL) water**
- ☐ **2 tablespoons caster sugar**
- ☐ **300 g watermelon, skinned, seeds removed and chopped**
- ☐ **250 g strawberries, hulled**
- ☐ **³/4 cup (190 mL) dry champagne (optional)**

1 Combine water and sugar in a saucepan and bring to the boil. Remove from heat and allow to cool completely.
2 In a food processor or blender puree watermelon flesh and strawberries.
3 Mix puree into sugar mixture and freeze in a stainless steel bowl. Whisk from time to time during freezing to give a smooth even texture. To serve, spoon into elegant glasses and at the last minute pour a tablespoon of champagne into each glass.

220 kilojoules (52 calories) per serve

Fat	0.1 g	low
Cholesterol	0 mg	low
Fibre	0.9 g	low
Sodium	4 mg	low

NUTRITION TIPS

✧ Dried fruit needs to be carefully counted by anyone with a weight problem. During drying, the fruit's water is largely removed which concentrates the kilojoules (calories) remaining.
✧ Remember: two dried apricots were originally one fresh apricot; one prune is equivalent to one plum; a handful of raisins is equivalent to a bunch of grapes.
✧ Apricots have the most concentrated dietary fibre of all dried fruit and supply vaulable amounts of iron, potassium, carotene, niacin and other B vitamins.

❖

FRUIT CAKE

No one would ever guess that our fruit cake has no eggs and so little fat. Yet it's a beautifully moist cake that's perfect for afternoon tea or lunch boxes.

Serves 16

- ☐ **³/4 cup (60 g) rice bran**
- ☐ **1 kg mixed dried fruit**
- ☐ **³/4 cup (130 g) brown sugar**
- ☐ **1 tablespoon grated orange rind**
- ☐ **4 tablespoons fresh orange juice**
- ☐ **6 tablespoons stout or beer**
- ☐ **³/4 cup (190 mL) hot water**
- ☐ **90 g melted polyunsaturated margarine (salt reduced)**
- ☐ **2 cups (270 g) wholemeal self-raising flour, sifted**
- ☐ **¹/2 teaspoon ground cinnamon**
- ☐ **¹/2 teaspoon ground ginger**
- ☐ **¹/2 teaspoon ground nutmeg**
- ☐ **¹/2 teaspoon ground cardamom**

1 Combine rice bran, dried fruit, brown sugar, orange rind, orange juice, 4 tablespoons of stout, and water in a bowl. Cool slightly, cover and stand overnight.
2 Stir in margarine, flour, cinnamon, ginger, nutmeg and cardamom. Spoon mixture into a lightly greased and lined 23 cm round cake pan. Bake for 1 ¹/2 hours at 150°C, or until cooked. Remove from oven, pour over remaining stout and wrap in aluminium foil until cool.

1295 kilojoules (295 calories) per serve

Fat	5.1 g	med
Cholesterol	0 mg	low
Fibre	6.7 g	high
Sodium	223 mg	med

❖

FRUITY COOKIES

As a treat these light fruity cookies will satisfy even the sweetest tooth.

Makes 16

- ☐ **60 g polyunsaturated margarine (salt reduced)**
- ☐ **4 tablespoons brown sugar**
- ☐ **2 tablespoons plain flour, sifted**
- ☐ **1 teaspoon mixed spice**
- ☐ **60 g finely chopped pecans**
- ☐ **1 tablespoon finely chopped glace cherries**
- ☐ **1 tablespoon currants**
- ☐ **1 tablespoon mixed peel**

1   Place margarine in a mixing bowl and beat until light and fluffy. Gradually add sugar and beat until just combined.
2   Fold in flour, mixed spice, pecans, cherries, currants and mixed peel. Place spoonfuls of mixture onto lightly greased oven trays, leaving 5 cm between each spoonful. It is best to cook only four biscuits at a time.
3   Bake at 180°C for 15 minutes or until golden brown. Remove from oven and using a spatula, push biscuits into a round shape and allow to cool on trays for 1–2 minutes. Transfer to a wire rack to cool.

296 kilojoules (71 calories) per serve

Fat	5.0 g	low
Cholesterol	0 mg	low
Fibre	0.3 g	low
Sodium	28 mg	low

ALMOND FRUIT BREAD

Perfect to serve with coffee, this adaptation of an old favourite is the ideal finish to any dinner party.

Serves 30

- ☐ **3 egg whites**
- ☐ **1 teaspoon almond essence**
- ☐ **1/2 cup (110 g) caster sugar**
- ☐ **1 cup (125 g) plain flour, sifted**
- ☐ **60 g slivered almonds**
- ☐ **125 g glace cherries, chopped**
- ☐ **60 g glace pineapple, chopped**
- ☐ **60 g glace apricots, chopped**
- ☐ **60 g glace ginger, chopped**

1   Beat egg whites and almond essence until soft peaks form. Add caster sugar, a spoonful at a time, beating well after each addition.
2   Fold in flour, almonds, cherries, pineapple, apricots and ginger. Spoon mixture into a lightly greased and lined 25 cm x 8 cm loaf pan. Bake at 180°C for 35–40 minutes or until firm.
3   Turn out onto a wire rack to cool completely. Wrap in aluminium foil and set aside for 1–2 days. Using a very sharp serrated knife, cut bread into wafer thin slices. Place slices onto an oven tray lined with baking paper and bake at 150°C for 35 minutes or until dry and crisp. Remove from oven and cool on wire rack.

227 kilojoules (54 calories) per serve

Fat	1.1 g	low
Cholesterol	0 mg	low
Fibre	0.6 g	low
Sodium	9 mg	low

D ID Y OU K NOW?

❖   Raisins and apricots are the oldest dried fruits and have been enjoyed by man since ancient times.
❖   Mention is made in the Old Testament of raisin cakes.
❖   It is known that apricots were being cultivated in China as long ago as 2205 BC.
❖   The Romans made a wine called Acinatisius from raisins and they were also a popular fruit at their banquets.

Garlic

Although scientific debate continues, more and more people are turning to garlic to keep their heart healthy. Large amounts of garlic, far in excess of that normally used in everyday cooking, have been shown to reduce the build up of fats in the blood after a fatty meal. Adding a little garlic to your cooking gives a wonderful flavour and aroma.

❖

TABBOULEH FILLED TOMATOES

Serves 4

☐ **4 large tomatoes**

TABBOULEH FILLING
☐ **3 tablespoons burghul (cracked wheat)**
☐ **boiling water**
☐ **8 shallots, finely chopped**
☐ **3 cloves garlic, crushed**
☐ **3 tablespoons finely chopped fresh parsley**
☐ **2 tablespoons finely chopped fresh mint**
☐ **1 tablespoon olive oil**
☐ **freshly ground black pepper**

1   Remove tops from tomatoes with a sharp knife. Scoop out pulp using a spoon, chop and reserve.
2   To make filling, place burghul in a bowl and pour over boiling water to cover. Set aside to soak for 10 minutes. Drain burghul and combine with tomato flesh, shallots, garlic, parsley, mint and oil. Season to taste with pepper. Spoon mixture into tomato shells and place on an oven tray. Bake at 200°C for 10 minutes or until heated through.

437 kilojoules (104 calories) per serve

Fat	4.9 g	low
Cholesterol	0 mg	low
Fibre	6.0 g	high
Sodium	13 mg	low

Tabbouleh Filled Tomatoes, Garlic Sesame Ginger Prawms

❖

GARLIC SESAME GINGER PRAWNS

This spicy stir-fry makes a delightful entree for a dinner party. As it is high in cholesterol, save it for special occasions.

Serves 8

☐ **1 teaspoon sesame oil**
☐ **1 kg uncooked prawns, shelled and deveined, tails left intact**
☐ **2 cloves garlic, crushed**
☐ **1 teaspoon grated fresh ginger**
☐ **2 tablespoons dry sherry**
☐ **³/4 cup (190 mL) beef stock**
☐ **2 teaspoons low salt soy sauce**
☐ **60 g canned pimento, finely chopped**
☐ **2 tablespoons finely chopped fresh chives**
☐ **1 tablespoon barbecue sauce (no added salt)**
☐ **3 teaspoons cornflour blended with 3 tablespoons water**
☐ **2 tablespoons toasted sesame seeds**

1   Heat oil in a non-stick frypan. Stir-fry prawns, garlic and ginger over high heat until prawns have just changed colour.
2   Stir in sherry, stock, soy sauce, pimento, chives and barbecue sauce. Simmer gently for 2–3 minutes. Add cornflour mixture and cook until sauce boils and thickens. Serve sprinkled with sesame seeds.

703 kilojoules (167 calories) per serve

Fat	4.5 g	low
Cholesterol	250 mg	high
Fibre	0.3 g	low
Sodium	528 mg	high

> ### COOK'S TIP
> To neutralise garlic's strong odour from your breath, try chewing fresh parsley. Cooked garlic is less offensive than raw.

Grains

Grains such as wheat, rice, oats, rye, barley, maize, millet and buckwheat have been the staple food of many people for centuries and for good reason: all are high in complex carbohydrate and fibre, with a good protein content and very little fat or salt. They are nourishing, satisfying foods that we should all include in generous quantities in our diet. Choosing from our flavoursome versions of favourite recipes, you'll have no difficulty enjoying these delicious foods each week.

❖

VEGETABLE SOUP

Hearty, delicious and nourishing, this soup is a complete meal in itself.

Serves 6

- ☐ 6 cups (1.5 litres) chicken stock
- ☐ ¹/₂ cup (100 g) pearl barley
- ☐ 2 tablespoons tomato paste (no added salt)
- ☐ 1 teaspoon mixed dried herbs
- ☐ 1 large onion, chopped
- ☐ 2 cloves garlic, crushed
- ☐ 2 stalks celery, sliced
- ☐ 2 large carrots, diced
- ☐ 1 parsnip, diced
- ☐ 1 small turnip, diced
- ☐ 200 g green beans, sliced

1   Place stock, barley, tomato paste and herbs in a large saucepan. Bring to the boil, reduce heat and simmer for 30 minutes.
2   Add onion, garlic, celery, carrots, parsnip, turnip and beans and cook for 20–25 minutes or until vegetables are tender.

496 kilojoules (111 calories) per serve

Fat	0.5 g	low
Cholesterol	0 mg	low
Fibre	5.3 g	high
Sodium	48 mg	low

❖

TUNA RICE RING

Quick and easy to prepare, this rice mould makes an attractive main course.

Serves 4

- ☐ 1 tablespoon olive oil
- ☐ 6 shallots, chopped
- ☐ 1 stalk celery, chopped
- ☐ 150 g button mushrooms, sliced
- ☐ 1 red capsicum, chopped
- ☐ 2 tablespoons chopped fresh parsley
- ☐ 3 cups (540 g) cooked brown rice
- ☐ 425 g canned chunk style tuna in spring water, drained
- ☐ 1 cup (45 g) rice bran
- ☐ 1 teaspoon chilli sauce
- ☐ 2 tomatoes, peeled and chopped
- ☐ freshly ground black pepper

1   Heat oil in a large frypan. Add shallots, celery, mushrooms and capsicum and cook for 2–3 minutes.
2   Stir in parsley, rice, tuna, rice bran, chilli sauce and half the tomatoes. Toss until heated through. Season to taste with pepper.
3   Spoon mixture into a lightly greased ring pan. Press down well. To serve, turn out onto a plate and top with remaining tomatoes. Serve hot or cold.

1902 kilojoules (458 calories) per serve

Fat	17.8 g	high
Cholesterol	35 mg	low
Fibre	7.2 g	high
Sodium	111 mg	low

DID YOU KNOW?

❖   Buckwheat is botanically a grass, but is usually included with the cereal grains because it is cooked and eaten in the same way. A part of the cuisines of Poland and Russia, buckwheat has a nutty flavour and is prepared in the same way as barley.

❖   Wild rice is not really rice at all but a grain from an aquatic grass which grows in North America. It has been a favourite food of North American Indians for hundreds of years. Wild rice has a pleasant nutty flavour and requires about 30 minutes' cooking, by which time the cooked grains should have burst.

SPINACH GNOCCHI

Gnocchi is an Italian favourite. It is easy to make yourself and our version has a herb sauce, which makes it a marvellous main course.

Serves 4

- ☐ 3 large potatoes, peeled and quartered
- ☐ 2 egg whites, lightly beaten
- ☐ 1 cup (170 g) semolina
- ☐ 250 g spinach, shredded and cooked
- ☐ freshly ground black pepper
- ☐ 2 tablespoons grated Parmesan cheese

SAUCE
- ☐ 1 ¹/₂ cups (375 mL) chicken stock
- ☐ 3 tablespoons dry white wine
- ☐ 1 cup (250 mL) evaporated skim milk
- ☐ 1 teaspoon French mustard
- ☐ 3 tablespoons grated Parmesan cheese
- ☐ 2 teaspoons polyunsaturated mayonnaise
- ☐ 1 teaspoon mixed dried herbs
- ☐ 2 tablespoons cornflour blended with ¹/₂ cup (125 mL) water
- ☐ freshly ground black pepper

1   Boil, steam or microwave potatoes. Drain well and mash. Add egg whites, semolina, spinach and pepper; mix to combine. Set aside to cool completely.
2   Turn out on a lightly floured board and knead briefly. Break off portions and roll into a sausage 1 cm diameter. Cut into 3 cm pieces. Press each piece lightly with a fork. Drop into a large saucepan of boiling water. Cook for 5 minutes or until gnocchi rises to the surface. Remove with a slotted spoon and keep warm.
3   To make sauce, bring stock, wine and evaporated milk to the boil. Mix in mustard, cheese, mayonnaise and herbs. Stir in cornflour mixture and bring back to the boil, stirring constantly. Simmer for 5 minutes and season to taste with pepper. To serve, place gnocchi on a warm serving plate, spoon over sauce and sprinkle with Parmesan cheese.

2025 kilojoules (483 calories) per serve

Fat	4.6 g	low
Cholesterol	10 mg	low
Fibre	11 g	high
Sodium	394 mg	high

Vegetable Soup, Tuna Rice Ring, Spinach Gnocchi

PUMPKIN WITH LEEK AND BEANS

Pumpkin with a difference, golden nuggets filled with a Middle Eastern flavoured stuffing.

Serves 4

☐ **2 golden nugget pumpkins**

FILLING
☐ **15 g burghul (cracked wheat)**
☐ **1 tablespoon olive oil**
☐ **2 cloves garlic, crushed**
☐ **1 small leek, thinly sliced**
☐ **50 g button mushrooms, sliced**
☐ **310 g canned red kidney beans, drained and rinsed**
☐ **1 tablespoon tomato sauce (no added salt)**
☐ **2 teaspoons Worcestershire sauce**
☐ **¹/₂ teaspoon chilli sauce**
☐ **³/₄ cup (90 g) grated mozzarella cheese**

1   Cut tops from pumpkin and scoop out seeds. Bake or microwave pumpkin until just tender. Drain and pat dry with absorbent kitchen paper. Transfer to a lightly greased tray.
2   To make filling, soak burghul in water for 30 minutes. Drain and set aside. Heat oil in a large frypan. Add garlic, leek and mushrooms, and cook over medium heat for 2–3 minutes.
3   Stir in beans, tomato sauce, Worcestershire sauce, chilli sauce and burghul. Toss to heat through.
4   Divide filling evenly between pumpkins. Sprinkle with cheese and bake at 180°C for 10 minutes or until cheese melts.

991 kilojoules (232 calories) per serve

Fat	*9.9 g*	*med*
Cholesterol	*16 mg*	*low*
Fibre	*1.2 g*	*med*
Sodium	*88 mg*	*low*

VEGETABLE AND RICE PATTIES

Serves 8

☐ **2 ¹/₂ cups (450 g) cooked brown rice**
☐ **³/₄ cup (30 g) unprocessed bran**
☐ **³/₄ cup (90 g) plain flour**
☐ **1 onion, grated**
☐ **1 clove garlic, crushed**
☐ **1 teaspoon grated fresh ginger**
☐ **1 cup (250 g) drained corn kernels**
☐ **1 carrot, grated**
☐ **1 zucchini, grated**
☐ **3 tablespoons toasted pine nuts**
☐ **2 tablespoons peanut butter**
☐ **2 teaspoons salt reduced soy sauce**
☐ **3 tablespoons low fat unflavoured yoghurt**
☐ **2 egg whites**
☐ **1 ¹/₂ cups (185 g) dry breadcrumbs**
☐ **2 tablespoons olive oil**

1   Combine rice, bran, flour, onion, garlic, ginger, corn, carrot, zucchini and pine nuts. Blend together peanut butter, soy sauce, yoghurt and egg whites and add to rice mixture.
2   Shape mixture into 16 patties. Coat with breadcrumbs. Heat a non-stick frypan and brush lightly with oil. Cook patties turning frequently until golden brown and cooked through.

1478 kilojoules (353 calories) per serve

Fat	*11.1 g*	*med*
Cholesterol	*0 mg*	*low*
Fibre	*4.6 g*	*high*
Sodium	*240 mg*	*med*

WILD RICE SALAD

Serves 6

☐ **100 g wild rice**
☐ **¹/₂ cup (100 g) long grain white rice**
☐ **¹/₂ cup (100 g) quick cooking brown rice**
☐ **3 tablespoons chopped fresh mint**
☐ **¹/₂ cup (60 g) toasted sunflower seeds**
☐ **2 tablespoons chopped glace ginger**
☐ **2 kiwi fruit, peeled and sliced**
☐ **¹/₂ cup (90 g) sultanas**

KIWI FRUIT DRESSING
☐ **2 kiwi fruit, peeled and chopped**
☐ **1 tablespoon polyunsaturated oil**
☐ **1 clove garlic, crushed**
☐ **1 teaspoon grated fresh ginger**
☐ **2 teaspoons honey**
☐ **1 teaspoon lemon juice**

1   Cook wild rice in a large pan of boiling water for 20–25 minutes or until grains burst. Add white and brown rice during last 12 minutes of cooking. Drain and set aside to cool.
2   Combine rice, mint, sunflower seeds, ginger, kiwi fruit and sultanas in a bowl.

3   To make dressing, place kiwi fruit, oil, garlic, ginger, honey and lemon juice in a food processor or blender. Process until smooth. Pour dressing over salad, toss and refrigerate until well chilled.

1051 kilojoules (250 calories) per serve

Fat	*7.8 g*	*med*
Cholesterol	*0 mg*	*low*
Fibre	*3.4 g*	*high*
Sodium	*25 mg*	*low*

THIRST QUENCHER
Barley water is a favourite summer time drink and is very easy to prepare. To make 1 litre of barley water, place 100 g pearl barley and 5 cups (1.25 litres) water in a saucepan with the rind of 2 large lemons. Bring to the boil and simmer for 20 minutes. Strain and stir in 3 tablespoons of caster sugar and the juice of 2 lemons. Chill before serving with a sprig of mint.

Pumpkin with Leek and Beans, Vegetable and Rice Patties, Wild Rice Salad

Honey

Many people believe honey to be superior to sugar, as it is a 'natural' sweetener with supposedly therapeutic benefits, such as the ability to ward off colds, arthritis and heart problems. Unfortunately, such claims do not always hold true. Honey consists of around 75 per cent sugars (half of which are glucose, half fructose), with small quantities of plant acids, gums, pigments and oils. It makes a pleasant alternative sweetening agent to sugar but has no medical advantages. It does contain small amounts of B vitamins and some minerals, but not in significant amounts. Like sugar, it supplies kilojoules which must be counted by anyone watching their weight. One tablespoon of honey supplies about 370 kilojoules (87 calories), which is about the same as one tablespoon of sugar. Enjoy it if you like its taste, but don't expect any miracles!

Ice Cream

With its saturated fat and cholesterol, ice cream is generally restricted on cholesterol-lowering diets. But there are several categories of 'ice cream' and in warm climates there is nothing more refreshing than a scoop of this icy cold smooth confection.

Water ices, gelato and low fat 'ice confections' have the least fat and are the best choices.

Standard ice cream (as sold in tubs in supermarkets) has around 10 percent of milk fat and is acceptable occasionally. Three scoops of a standard vanilla ice cream supply 574 kilojoules (137 calories) and 7 grams of fat.

Premium ice creams, sold by exclusive confectionery outlets, have the highest fat content of 15–16 per cent and are denser which is why they taste richer and smoother.

Try our Watermelon and Strawberry Sorbet (page 33), which is also delicious made using 500 g of apricots in place of the watermelon and strawberries.

Jelly

For a delicious low cholesterol dessert that children will love don't forget jelly. It can be a refreshing fat free dessert, whether you use a commercial packet or make your own from pureed fruit or juices and gelatine. While a packet mix is largely sugar, gelatine and flavouring, it has no fat, is convenient and appreciated by children. There are low kilojoule jelly mixes for those wishing to avoid sugar or cut kilojoules.

All you need to do to make your own fresh fruit jelly is dissolve 4 teaspoons gelatine in 4 tablespoons water and mix with 600 mL fresh fruit juice. Do not use fresh pineapple or pawpaw juice because enzymes present in these juices prevent the jelly from setting.

Kilojoules

(Calories)

Kilojoules are units used to measure the energy of foods or diets. As metric units, kilojoules are replacing kilocalories (often called simply calories) in research and teaching. To convert kilojoules to calories, divide by 4.186 (4.2 or just 4 is accurate enough for a quick conversion). Most women eat an average of 7500 kilojoules (1800 calories) a day and a sensible weight loss plan should be no less than 4000 to 5000 kilojoules (1000 to 1200 calories) a day.

Spicy Vegetable Loaf, Vegetables with Almond Curry

Legumes

Lentils, dried peas, and beans (known collectively as pulses or legumes) are excellent foods to include in a cholesterol-lowering diet. They have very little fat, no cholesterol, and substantial amounts of protein, which is useful for vegetarians. Most importantly, they offer a good fibre content, high in water-soluble fibre, which helps remove cholesterol from the body, in a similar way to oat bran.

The initial step of presoaking beans often deters people from using dried beans. Lentils are the most convenient, requiring no pre-soaking to soften before cooking. Alternatively, canned beans are quick and nutritious. There is some loss of B vitamins during canning, but this is not significant. A couple of cans of beans in your cupboard is always handy for an easy, no-fuss high fibre meal.

❖

SPICY VEGETABLE LOAF

Serves 6

- ☐ 1 tablespoon olive oil
- ☐ 1 clove garlic, crushed
- ☐ 1 onion, finely chopped
- ☐ $^1/_2$ teaspoon chilli powder
- ☐ $^1/_2$ teaspoon ground cumin
- ☐ $^1/_2$ teaspoon ground coriander
- ☐ $^1/_2$ teaspoon ground turmeric
- ☐ 2 $^1/_4$ cups (450 g) red lentils
- ☐ 1 carrot, grated
- ☐ 1 large potato, grated
- ☐ 400 g canned tomatoes (no added salt), undrained and mashed
- ☐ 2 cups (500 mL) vegetable stock
- ☐ 1 $^1/_2$ cups (135 g) rolled oats
- ☐ 3 egg whites
- ☐ freshly ground black pepper

1   Heat oil in a large frypan and cook garlic, onion, chilli powder, cumin, coriander and turmeric for 4–5 minutes or until onion softens.

2   Add lentils, carrot, potato, tomatoes and stock. Bring to the boil, cover and simmer for 30 minutes or until lentils are tender. Remove from heat and set aside to cool slightly. Beat egg whites until stiff peaks form and fold into lentil mixture.

3   Stir in rolled oats and mix well to combine. Season to taste with pepper. Spoon into a lightly greased and lined 15 cm x 25 cm loaf pan. Bake at 180°C for 1 hour or until cooked.

918 kilojoules (219 calories) per serve

Fat	5.0 g	low
Cholesterol	0 mg	low
Fibre	5.0 g	high
Sodium	27 mg	low

❖

VEGETABLES WITH ALMOND CURRY

Serves 4

- ☐ 1 tablespoon olive oil
- ☐ 1 onion, sliced
- ☐ 1 clove garlic, crushed
- ☐ 1 teaspoon ground cumin
- ☐ 1 teaspoon ground coriander
- ☐ 1 teaspoon ground turmeric
- ☐ 2 carrots, peeled and sliced
- ☐ $^1/_2$ cup (110 g) red lentils
- ☐ 440 g canned peeled tomatoes (no added salt), undrained
- ☐ 1 $^1/_2$ cups (375 mL) vegetable stock
- ☐ 1 teaspoon chilli sauce or according to taste
- ☐ 500 g pumpkin, peeled and cut into 2 cm cubes
- ☐ $^1/_2$ cauliflower, cut into florets
- ☐ 2 tablespoons blanched almonds
- ☐ freshly ground black pepper
- ☐ 4 tablespoons unflavoured low fat yoghurt

1   Brush a large saucepan with olive oil, heat and cook onion, garlic, cumin, coriander, turmeric and carrots for 5 minutes or until onion softens.

2   Stir in lentils, tomatoes and stock. Bring to the boil, reduce heat, cover and simmer for 15 minutes.

3   Add chilli sauce, pumpkin and cauliflower. Cook for 15–20 minutes longer or until pumpkin is tender. Mix in almonds and season to taste with pepper. Ladle curry into bowls and top with a spoonful of yoghurt.

818 kilojoules (194 calories) per serve

Fat	6.6 g	med
Cholesterol	0 mg	low
Fibre	5.2 g	high
Sodium	62 mg	low

LENTIL SALAD

Serves 6

- ☐ **1 cup (200 g) red lentils**
- ☐ **1 cup (200 g) yellow lentils**
- ☐ **6 cups (1.5 litres) vegetable stock**
- ☐ **1 teaspoon cumin seeds**
- ☐ **2 tomatoes, diced**
- ☐ **2 stalks celery, sliced**
- ☐ **¹/₂ small green capsicum, diced**
- ☐ **¹/₂ small red capsicum, diced**
- ☐ **1 small onion, finely chopped**
- ☐ **1 small avocado, chopped**
- ☐ **freshly ground black pepper**
- ☐ **2 tablespoons chopped chives**

1   Place lentils, stock and cumin seeds in a saucepan and bring to the boil. Reduce heat and simmer for 20 minutes or until lentils are tender. Drain and allow to cool.
2   In a large salad bowl place cold lentils, tomatoes, celery, green and red capsicum, onion and avocado.
3   To make dressing, in a screwtop jar combine coriander, turmeric, chilli powder, garlic, vinegar and oil. Shake well to combine and pour over salad. Toss and season to taste with pepper. Sprinkle with chives to serve.

526 kilojoules (126 calories) per serve

Fat	8.2 g	*med*
Cholesterol	0 mg	*low*
Fibre	3.2 g	*high*
Sodium	20 mg	*low*

Below: Lentil Salad, Red Hot Beans

Knowing Your Legumes – from top left:

borlotte beans
red lentils
lima beans
kidney beans
green split beans
chick peas
cannellini beans
brown lentils

NUTRITION TIPS

✧ Legumes are often avoided because they cause embarrassing flatulence (wind). This can be considerably reduced by discarding the soaking water, rinsing beans, and adding fresh water for cooking. The flatulence is caused by certain food components in legumes, which are not fully digested, and end up being broken down to gases in the bowel.
✧ Legumes supply valuable amounts of B group vitamins, especially vitamin B, B6, niacin, and folic acid. They are also a good source of the minerals calcium, potassium and phosphorus. Their iron content is fairly high, but occurs in an inorganic form, not well absorbed by the human body. Eating a food high in vitamin C (like orange juice or a salad) at the same meal as legumes, increases the absorption of the iron.

❖

RED HOT BEANS

The hotness of these Red Hot Beans can be altered according to taste. If you are unsure, carefully add a little chilli sauce, tasting until it is right. Serve with bowls of unflavoured low fat yoghurt. These beans make a wonderful main course.

Serves 4

- ☐ ³/₄ **cup (125 g) dry red kidney beans**
- ☐ **1 eggplant, diced**
- ☐ **1 red capsicum, cut into strips**
- ☐ **1 large onion, sliced**
- ☐ **1 clove garlic, crushed**
- ☐ **4 large tomatoes, skinned and roughly chopped**
- ☐ **2 tablespoons tomato puree (no added salt)**
- ☐ **2 teaspoons chilli sauce**
- ☐ ¹/₂ **cup (125 mL) water**
- ☐ **freshly ground black pepper**
- ☐ **2 tablespoons chopped fresh coriander**

1   Soak beans in water overnight, then drain well.

2   In a large saucepan place beans, eggplant, capsicum, onion, garlic, tomatoes, tomato puree, chilli sauce and water. Bring to the boil and boil rapidly for 10 minutes. Reduce heat and simmer, stirring occasionally, for 1 hour or until beans are tender.

3   Season with pepper and sprinkle with coriander to serve.

1245 kilojoules (293 calories) per serve		
Fat	1.7 g	low
Cholesterol	0 mg	low
Fibre	27.4 g	high
Sodium	60 mg	low

TIMESAVERS

❖   When cooking beans, cook extra as these can be frozen and added to dishes as required.

❖   While pulses are usually soaked overnight and this is preferable there is a way to speed up the soaking process if necessary. Place pulses in unsalted water, bring to the boil and simmer for 5 minutes, remove from heat and stand for 1 hour. Drain, rinse and use as required.

---

10 WAYS TO LOW FAT COOKING

One of the easiest ways to reduce the amount of fat you eat is to use less fat when you cook.

1   Avoid frying in oil, butter, margarine or ghee. Instead stick to grilling, roasting on a rack, steaming or microwave cooking. Try wrapping in foil and baking, or stir-frying in stock for a change.

2   Always trim all visible fat from meat; remove fat and skin from chicken. At the butcher's or supermarket, look for lean meat with the least fat and marbling. Limit the amount of sausages, luncheon meats and salamis you eat.

3   Use a non-stick frypan and simply brush with a little oil (don't pour oil in) for browning and sauteing.

4   Change the emphasis of your meals. Eat more pasta, rice, vegetables, bread and fruit, and less meat and fatty sauces.

5   Cook casseroles and soups one day ahead and chill. Any fat will rise to the surface and can be easily removed once it solidifies.

6   Experiment with vegetarian recipes. Replace some meat in casseroles with lentils and dried beans.

7   Baste foods with wine, oil free marinade, stock or fruit juice – not oil.

8   Use low fat or skim milk in cooking whenever possible. Switch to cottage cheese or ricotta in place of cream cheese and sour cream. Experiment with less butter and margarine in cake and biscuit recipes.

9   Indulge in gelato or fruit sorbets instead of ice cream.

10   Try non fat, unflavoured yoghurt in place of sour cream to finish casseroles. Do not reboil, as the yoghurt will look curdled.

Meats

Lean meats, whether red or white, can be part of a healthy low cholesterol way of eating provided that all visible fat is trimmed away and the cooking method does not add extra fats. Recent analyses show that if meat is not 'marbled' almost all the fat lies between muscles and is easy to remove. Hence lean beef, lamb and pork can now all be incorporated into family meals and provide all-important nutrition and flavour. Fat-trimmed meat is an excellent source of protein (containing all the amino acids needed for growth and health), iron and B vitamins. Sample our mouth-watering meat dishes and you'll be surprised at how easy and tasty lean meat cooking can be.

BEEF WITH MUSTARD AND ROSEMARY

Great for mid-week entertaining this easy main course dish takes next to no time to prepare.

Serves 4

- ☐ **600 g whole lean beef fillet**
- ☐ **2 teaspoons French mustard**
- ☐ **2 tablespoons cracked peppercorns**
- ☐ **1 tablespoon polyunsaturated oil**

SAUCE
- ☐ **1 clove garlic**
- ☐ **2 teaspoons chopped fresh rosemary**
- ☐ **1 teaspoon grated lemon rind**
- ☐ **1/2 cup (125 mL) dry white wine**
- ☐ **1/4 cup (60 mL) evaporated skim milk**
- ☐ **1 teaspoon cornflour**

1   Trim all visible fat from meat. Spread mustard over all surfaces of meat. Coat with peppercorns.

2   Heat oil in a roasting pan. Add meat and sear well on all sides. Transfer pan to oven and bake at 180°C for 20–25 minutes. Remove meat from pan. Set aside and keep warm.

3   To make sauce, skim any fat from pan. Place pan on stove top and stir in garlic, rosemary and lemon rind. Cook for 1–2 minutes.

4   Pour in wine and cook over high heat, stirring frequently to lift sediment from base of pan. Reduce wine by half. Combine skim milk and cornflour, stir into wine mixture. Cook over medium heat until sauce thickens slightly. Slice beef and spoon over sauce to serve.

1078 kilojoules (258 calories) per serve

Fat	10.5 g	med
Cholesterol	101 mg	high
Fibre	0 g	low
Sodium	163 mg	med

FAT FIGHTER

Cook meat with as little extra fat as possible. Do not fry or roast in fat. Instead grill, dry-bake on a rack, barbecue, microwave or cook in a non-stick pan brushed with a little oil. For casseroles, brown meat first in a touch of oil, then remove from pan and continue cooking other ingredients. Sour cream can often be replaced with plain yoghurt, but remember not to boil or the casserole will look curdled.

STEAKS WITH GARLIC TOMATO CONCASSE

For a change try our concasse with lamb chops or chicken fillets.

Serves 6

- ☐ **6 x 120 g boneless rib-eye steaks (scotch fillet)**

GARLIC TOMATO CONCASSE
- ☐ **4 large tomatoes, peeled and chopped**
- ☐ **2 cloves garlic, crushed**
- ☐ **2 tablespoons finely chopped chives**
- ☐ **freshly ground black pepper**

1 To make concasse, place tomatoes, garlic and chives in a saucepan. Cook over medium heat for 8–10 minutes or until tomatoes are just soft. Season to taste with pepper.

2 Trim all visible fat from meat. Heat a non-stick frypan and cook steaks over medium-high heat for 4–5 minutes each side. Spoon sauce over steaks and serve immediately.

799 kilojoules (192 calories) per serve

Fat	*5.3 g*	*med*
Cholesterol	*80 mg*	*med*
Fibre	*3.3 g*	*high*
Sodium	*62 mg*	*low*

Low Fat Roasts

To enjoy the full flavour of a traditional roast cook the roast on a rack. In this way the meat does not absorb the fat that is released during cooking. To avoid splattering during cooking, place a cup of water in the pan. To make gravy, use the pan juices and at the end of cooking, throw a handful of ice cubes into the pan and stir until melted. You will see the fat solidify on the surface, remove it using a slotted spoon and make your gravy as usual.

Above: Athenian Lamb Kebabs
Left: Beef with Mustard and Rosemary, Steaks with Garlic Tomato Concasse

ATHENIAN LAMB KEBABS

Our Mediterranean-flavoured kebabs will quickly become a family favourite.

Serves 6

- ☐ **750 g lean lamb, cubed and trimmed of fat**
- ☐ **12 bay leaves**
- ☐ **1 large onion, cut into eighths**
- ☐ **12 cherry tomatoes**
- ☐ **1 green capsicum, cubed**

MARINADE
- ☐ **1 tablespoon olive oil**
- ☐ **3 tablespoons lemon juice**
- ☐ **1 teaspoon finely chopped fresh rosemary**
- ☐ **3 tablespoons finely chopped fresh parsley**
- ☐ **fresh ground black pepper**
- ☐ **dash Tabasco sauce**

1 To make marinade, combine oil, lemon juice, rosemary, parsley, pepper to taste and Tabasco sauce in a glass bowl. Add meat, toss to coat and marinate for 30 minutes.

2 Remove meat from marinade and thread on to twelve oiled wooden skewers, alternating with bay leaves, onion, tomatoes and capsicum.

3 Barbecue or grill kebabs slowly, turning and basting frequently with remaining marinade, until well browned and cooked.

798 kilojoules (192 calories) per serve

Fat	*7.2 g*	*med*
Cholesterol	*83 mg*	*med*
Fibre	*0.9 g*	*low*
Sodium	*103 mg*	*low*

PORK WITH ORANGE AND CRANBERRY

Butterfly pork steaks with their lean meaty quality, are excellent with this tasty sauce.

Serves 4

- ☐ **4 x 125 g lean butterfly pork steaks**
- ☐ **cracked black peppercorns**
- ☐ **1 teaspoon grape seed oil**

MARINADE
- ☐ **1 cup (250 mL) fresh orange juice**
- ☐ **2 teaspoons grated orange rind**
- ☐ **$^1/_4$ teaspoon ground cloves**
- ☐ **3 tablespoons cranberry sauce**

1 Trim all visible fat from meat. To make marinade, combine orange juice, orange rind, cloves and cranberry sauce in a glass bowl. Add meat and marinate for 1–2 hours.

2 Remove steaks from marinade and coat with peppercorns. Heat oil in a non-stick frypan. Cook steaks for 4–5 minutes each side or until cooked. Set aside and keep warm.

3 Strain remaining marinade and pour into a saucepan. Bring to the boil and boil rapidly to reduce slightly. Spoon sauce over steaks and serve.

911 kilojoules (218 calories) per serve

Fat	*2.4 g*	*low*
Cholesterol	*68 mg*	*med*
Fibre	*0 g*	*low*
Sodium	*70 mg*	*low*

NUTRITION TIP

Red or white meat? It seems that the colour of cooked meat has no bearing on its fat and cholesterol content. Some of the leanest meats such as venison, buffalo and kangaroo are deep red in colour and their very lack of fat has made them more difficult to cook without becoming tough!

MOUSSAKA WITH CRUNCHY TOPPING

Great for casual entertaining. Prepare and cook this tasty moussaka in advance, then all you need do is reheat when you are ready to serve.

Serves 4

- ☐ **1 onion, chopped**
- ☐ **2 cloves garlic, crushed**
- ☐ **500 g lean minced beef**
- ☐ **1 teaspoon chopped fresh rosemary**
- ☐ **400 g canned tomatoes (no added salt), undrained and mashed**
- ☐ **2 tablespoons tomato paste (no added salt)**
- ☐ **2 teaspoons low salt soy sauce**
- ☐ **$^1/_2$ cup (125 mL) dry red wine**
- ☐ **1 teaspoon sugar**
- ☐ **$^1/_4$ teaspoon ground nutmeg**
- ☐ **1 eggplant, thinly sliced**
- ☐ **6 slices wholemeal bread, crusts removed**
- ☐ **1 tablespoon polyunsaturated margarine**
- ☐ **2 tablespoons finely chopped fresh basil**
- ☐ **1 tablespoon grated Parmesan cheese**

1 Heat a non-stick frypan. Cook onion, garlic, mince and rosemary over medium heat for 4–5 minutes, stirring constantly.

2 Stir in tomatoes, tomato paste, soy sauce, wine, sugar and nutmeg. Cook, uncovered, over medium heat for 20–25 minutes or until mixture reduces and thickens slightly.

3 Steam or microwave eggplant for 2–3 minutes. Arrange layers of eggplant and mince mixture in a 16 cm x 28 cm lightly greased ovenproof dish, finishing with a layer of mince.

4 Spread bread slices with margarine and cut into large cubes. Place on top of moussaka. Sprinkle with basil and Parmesan cheese, bake at 180°C for 30–35 minutes.

1534 kilojoules (367 calories) per serve

Fat	*10.6 g*	*med*
Cholesterol	*64 mg*	*med*
Fibre	*5.1 g*	*high*
Sodium	*423 mg*	*high*

Left: Pork with Orange and Cranberry
Right: Moussaka with Crunchy Topping,
Hungarian Ragout.

HUNGARIAN RAGOUT

In our tasty ragout the meat is gently simmered giving a hearty and wholesome dish.

Serves 4

- [ ] **500 g lean stewing veal**
- [ ] **1 tablespoon polyunsaturated oil**
- [ ] **1 large onion, finely chopped**
- [ ] **1 clove garlic, crushed**
- [ ] **125 g button mushrooms, sliced**
- [ ] **2 teaspoons ground paprika**
- [ ] **$^1/_2$ teaspoon dried caraway seeds**
- [ ] **2 large tomatoes, peeled and chopped**
- [ ] **1 tablespoon tomato paste (no added salt)**
- [ ] **$^3/_4$ cup (190 mL) chicken stock**
- [ ] **3 tablespoons dry white wine**
- [ ] **freshly ground black pepper**
- [ ] **1 tablespoon cornflour blended with $^1/_2$ cup (125 g) low fat unflavoured yoghurt**

1   Trim meat of all visible fat. Cut into 2.5 cm cubes and set aside.

2   Heat oil in a large saucepan. Cook onion, garlic and mushrooms for 2–3 minutes. Add meat and cook for 3–4 minutes, tossing until browned on all sides.

3   Add paprika and caraway seeds and toss through meat mixture. Combine tomatoes, tomato paste, stock and wine and pour into pan. Season to taste with pepper. Bring to the boil, reduce heat and simmer covered for 1$^1/_2$ hours or until meat is tender.

4   Remove pan from heat and whisk in cornflour mixture. Cook over low heat for 3–4 minutes or until sauce thickens.

897 kilojoules (215 calories) per serve

Fat	6.0 g	med
Cholesterol	93 mg	med
Fibre	3.9 g	high
Sodium	127 mg	low

LIVER

✧ Liver and other offal or organ meats (kidney, heart, brains, tongue, tripe and sweetbreads) have a very high cholesterol count and are often excluded when trying to reduce blood cholesterol levels. However, provided you keep your saturated fat intake low and you do not have a 'cholesterol sensitive' biochemistry, offal meats can be eaten occasionally (say, once a week).

✧ All offal is nutritious, being an excellent food for iron, zinc, B vitamins, vitamin A and protein. Liver was once regularly fed to pregnant women and people suffering anaemia, for its exceptionally rich iron content. Brains have the highest cholesterol content (three times as concentrated as eggs) followed by liver and kidneys. The others are much lower.

Milk

One of our basic foods, milk, has excellent nutritional benefits, being rich in bone-building calcium and phosphorus and high in protein and B vitamins (particularly riboflavin or vitamin B2). Full cream milk, however, contributes much saturated fat and cholesterol, so skim and fat reduced 'modified' milks are recommended for those trying to lower their blood cholesterol.

Honey Banana Smoothie , Strawberry Flip

STRAWBERRY FLIP

Feeling hungry? Our flip is the ideal snack and you can use any berries you like.

Serves 2

- [ ] **100 g fresh strawberries, hulled**
- [ ] **1 cup (250 mL) skim milk**
- [ ] **2 tablespoons orange juice**

Place strawberries, skim milk and orange juice into a food processor or blender. Process until smooth. Serve immediately.

247 kilojoules (58 calories) per serve

Fat	0.2 g	low
Cholesterol	3 mg	low
Fibre	1.2 g	med
Sodium	69 mg	low

HONEY BANANA SMOOTHIE

Sure to last you until lunchtime, our thick smoothie is great for a quick breakfast. Try it with your favourite fruits.

Serves 4

- [ ] **2 large ripe bananas, chopped**
- [ ] **2 $^1/_2$ cups (625 mL) skim milk**
- [ ] **1 cup (250 mL) evaporated skim milk, chilled**
- [ ] **$^1/_2$ teaspoon cinnamon**
- [ ] **1 $^1/_2$ tablespoons honey**

Place bananas, both milks, cinnamon and honey in a food processor or blender. Process until thick and smooth.

919 kilojoules (217 calories) per serve

Fat	0.4 g	low
Cholesterol	5 mg	low
Fibre	2.0 g	med
Sodium	146 mg	low

WHICH MILK?

Most milks carry a nutrition information label on the side of their package which can help you decide the best type to buy, as there are differing names for similar types of milk in different areas.

Skim milk has had virtually all fat and cholesterol removed, while retaining a full complement of calcium, protein and minerals. It has the least fat and kilojoules of all milks, but has a thin 'watery' feel in the mouth.

Modified low fat milks have a fat content similar to skim milk but with added calcium, protein and lactose. This gives them a 'richer' taste than skim milk.

Modified reduced fat milks have around half the fat and cholesterol of regular milk, but with a creamy taste, which most people find quite acceptable.

Soya bean milks are suitable for children who have an allergy to the protein in cow's milk or for people unable to digest lactose (milk sugar), but are not always a good substitute. Although they are free of cholesterol, they can contain just as much fat as full cream milk and, unless fortified with added calcium, are not as rich in calcium.

MILK FATS	
MILK TYPE	FAT CONTENT
Full cream	4%
Reduced fat modified	1.5 – 2%
Low fat modified	0.15%
Skim	0.1%

❖

CREAMY ASPARAGUS SOUP

A swirl of unflavoured natural yoghurt and freshly chopped chives make a wonderful garnish for this flavoursome soup.

Serves 4

- ☐ **420 g canned asparagus cuts (no added salt)**
- ☐ **1 ¹/2 cups (375 mL) chicken stock**
- ☐ **2 tablespoons chopped fresh chives**
- ☐ **1 clove garlic, crushed**
- ☐ **pinch ground nutmeg**
- ☐ **1 cup (250 mL) skim milk**
- ☐ **freshly ground black pepper**

1   Drain asparagus reserving ¹/2 cup (125 mL) of liquid. Place asparagus cuts, reserved liquid, stock, chives, garlic and nutmeg in a food processor or blender. Process until smooth.
2   Transfer mixture to a saucepan. Bring to the boil, reduce heat and stir in skim milk. Heat gently, without boiling. Season to taste with pepper.

139 kilojoules (33 calories) per serve

Fat	*0.4 g*	*low*
Cholesterol	*0 mg*	*low*
Fibre	*0.8 g*	*low*
Sodium	*38 mg*	*low*

Creamy Asparagus Soup

Nuts

In small amounts, nuts add a wonderful flavour and aroma to your cooking. They are restricted because their high natural content of oil makes them high in fat and kilojoules (calories). Also, they are so "more-ish", it's often difficult to stop crunching, which creates a problem for anyone trying to shed excess weight. Certain nuts are preferred because of their richer content of unsaturated fats. We have used these to create the following deliciously nutty recipes. They're sure to be winners with your family and friends.

CONSUME WITH CARE

✧ To increase the flavour of nuts, try them roasted – but not in fat! Simply place on a baking tray and heat in the oven at 180°C for 5 minutes, shaking the tray once or twice. Take care not to burn – remove when just golden. Sesame, sunflower and pumpkin seeds can also be roasted in the same way.

✧ Try roasting nuts in the microwave. Place 250 g nuts in a microwave-safe glass or ceramic dish and cook on HIGH (100%) for 2–3 minutes. Do not add any oil or fat or they will burn.

✧ Nuts contain around half their weight as fat, which means they carry more fat than fatty meat or even cream! Make sure you use them cautiously. Coconut has the highest content of saturated fat (94%), followed by cashews at 20%, the rest are predominantly polyunsaturated or monounsaturated. Nuts contain no cholesterol.

PEANUT SAUCE

Peanut sauce is great served with vegetables, meat, chicken or fish. We have served ours with vegetable crudites making a great nibbles tray for a party.

Makes 1 cup (250 mL)

- [ ] **1 clove garlic, crushed**
- [ ] **1 onion, chopped**
- [ ] **1 teaspoon chilli sauce**
- [ ] **5 tablespoons crunchy peanut butter (no added salt)**
- [ ] **1/2 cup (125 mL) water**
- [ ] **1/2 cup (125 mL) low fat yoghurt**
- [ ] **freshly ground black pepper**

Cook garlic and onion in a non-stick frypan until onion softens. Add chilli sauce, peanut butter and water. Mix well to combine and bring to a gentle boil. Stir in yoghurt and season to taste with pepper.

271 kilojoules (65 calories) per serve

Fat	4.7 g	low
Cholesterol	0 mg	low
Fibre	0.3 g	low
Sodium	10 mg	low

SPICED ALMONDS

Serves 6

- [ ] **1/2 teaspoon chilli powder**
- [ ] **1/4 teaspoon ground cumin**
- [ ] **1/2 teaspoon ground coriander**
- [ ] **1 cup (160 g) blanched almonds**

1   Place chilli, cumin and coriander in a non-stick saucepan. Cook over low heat for 1 minute. Add almonds and toss with spices and cook for a further 3–5 minutes or until golden.

2   Remove pan from heat and set aside to cool. Serve as a snack or with drinks.

623 kilojoules (151 calories) per serve

Fat	14.3 g	low
Cholesterol	0 mg	low
Fibre	3.8 g	high
Sodium	2 mg	low

Left: Knowing your nuts – from top left:
macadamia, pecans, cashews, walnuts, brazils, pistachios, peanuts, almonds, pinenuts, sesame seeds

Peanut Sauce, Spiced Almonds

NUTTY NUTRITION			
NUT	POLY-UNSATURATED %	MONO-UNSATURATED %	SATURATED %
Almonds	22	68	10
Brazil nuts	38	36	10
Coconut, desiccated	1	5	94
Cashews	18	62	20
Chestnuts	42	39	18
Hazelnuts	10	81	8
Macadamias	2	82	16
Peanuts	33	52	15
Pecans	26	66	8
Pinenuts	44	40	16
Walnuts	66	24	9
Expressed as % of total fatty acids			

Oats

In recent years, oats have risen in prominence after nutrition research showed that they have a natural ability to lower blood cholesterol. From their humble beginnings as a peasant food, they are today considered a valuable 'health' food to eat daily, whether as porridge (rolled oats), muesli, oat muffins or in many other tempting dishes.

Oat bran is oat fibre in concentrated form, being the outer layers of the oat grain. It is high in soluble fibre, which nutritionists presently believe to be responsible for removing cholesterol from the body as well as delaying absorption of food (especially helpful for diabetics). Rolled oats also contain oat bran, as it is part of the oat grain, but in smaller quantities.

Three tablespoons (30 g) of oat bran gives you 5 grams of dietary fibre and 445 kilojoules (105 calories).

To have a significant effect on cholesterol you need to consume 60 to 100 g per day as well as modifying the fats in your diet.

❖

BANANA AND PINEAPPLE MUFFINS

Makes 12

- ☐ 1 ¹/4 cups (165 g) wholemeal self-raising flour
- ☐ 1 teaspoon baking powder
- ☐ 1 teaspoon mixed spice
- ☐ 4 tablespoons brown sugar
- ☐ 1 cup (45 g) oat bran
- ☐ 1 small banana, mashed
- ☐ 150 g canned crushed pineapple, drained
- ☐ 3 egg whites, lightly beaten
- ☐ 2 tablespoons polyunsaturated oil
- ☐ ¹/2 cup (125 mL) pineapple juice

1 Sift flour, baking powder and spice into a mixing bowl. Add sugar and oat bran.

2 Make a well in the centre of the dry ingredients. Combine banana, pineapple, egg whites, oil and juice. Stir into flour mixture and mix to combine all ingredients.

3 Spoon mixture into lightly greased muffin pans. Bake at 200°C for 12–15 minutes or until golden brown.

505 kilojoules (120 calories) per serve

Fat	3.2 g	low
Cholesterol	0 mg	low
Fibre	2.5 g	med
Sodium	139 mg	low

❖

FRESH HERB AND OAT SCONES

Make these delicious scones in advance. Freeze them and reheat just before serving.

Makes 9

- ☐ 1 ¹/2 cups (185 g) self-raising flour, sifted
- ☐ ¹/2 cup (45 g) instant oats
- ☐ ¹/2 teaspoon baking powder
- ☐ 30 g polyunsaturated margarine
- ☐ 2 teaspoons chopped fresh parsley
- ☐ 2 teaspoons chopped fresh basil
- ☐ 2 teaspoons chopped fresh rosemary
- ☐ ³/4 cup (190 mL) skim milk

1 Place flour, oats and baking powder in a bowl. Rub through margarine until mixture resembles fine breadcrumbs. Stir in parsley, basil and rosemary.

2 Make a well in the centre of mixture and pour in milk. Mix lightly with a knife until all ingredients are just combined. Turn mixture out onto a lightly floured board and knead lightly.

3 Press dough out evenly to 2 cm thickness. Cut into rounds using a 5 cm cutter dipped in flour. Arrange scones side by side in a lightly greased 18 cm round shallow cake pan. Brush tops with a little extra milk and bake at 220°C for 15–20 minutes or until scones are a golden brown.

486 kilojoules (115 calories) per serve

Fat	3.6 g	low
Cholesterol	0 mg	low
Fibre	2.3 g	med
Sodium	211 mg	med

CHEESY APPLE MUFFINS

Makes 12

- ☐ 1 ¹/₄ cups (165 g) wholemeal self-raising flour
- ☐ ¹/₄ teaspoon ground cinnamon
- ☐ ¹/₄ teaspoon ground nutmeg
- ☐ ¹/₄ teaspoon ground ginger
- ☐ ¹/₄ teaspoon ground cloves
- ☐ 1 teaspoon baking powder
- ☐ 1 cup (45 g) oat bran
- ☐ 3 tablespoons brown sugar
- ☐ 1 green apple, peeled and grated
- ☐ 125 g ricotta cheese
- ☐ 2 tablespoons polyunsaturated oil
- ☐ ³/₄ cup (190 mL) apple juice

1   Sift flour, cinnamon, nutmeg, ginger, cloves and baking powder into a mixing bowl. Add oat bran and sugar.

2   Make a well in the centre of the flour mixture. Stir in apple, ricotta, oil and apple juice. Mix until just combined. Spoon mixture into lightly greased muffin pans.

Bake at 200°C for 25 minutes or until golden brown.

495 kilojoules (118 calories) per serve

Fat	*4.4 g*	*low*
Cholesterol	*5 mg*	*low*
Fibre	*2.4 g*	*med*
Sodium	*147 mg*	*low*

FAT FIGHTER

Most muesli consists of one half rolled oats, the other half dried fruit, nuts and seeds. Plain non-toasted muesli is a nutritious easy breakfast and can be made at home from your own ingredients. Take care with toasted muesli, much of which has twice as much fat from the oil used during toasting. It is usually saturated and not good for your heart.
✧   Look for 'low in fat' brands with no saturated fat.

DID YOU KNOW?

✧   Oats were first cultivated in Europe in about 1000 BC and became well established in cold damp climates such as Scotland and Scandinavia, where other grains could not survive. They have long been used as a feed for animals and were often considered a 'poor man's food' as they were cheap and filling.

✧   Muesli was first first developed by a Swiss doctor, Dr Bircher-Benner, in his Zurich sanatorium in the 1890s. Rolled oats were soaked in water overnight and then a whole apple grated over the top. It was served with chopped nuts and yoghurt or cream. A far cry from today's muesli mixes!

Left: Banana and Pineapple Muffins, Cheesy Apple Muffins
Right: Fresh Herb and Oat Scones

Oils

Oils play a vital part in a cholesterol-lowering diet as they can influence the proportion of saturated, monounsaturated and polyunsaturated fat you eat. In a stir-fried vegetable dish the only fat is derived from whichever oil is selected for cooking. If it is peanut oil, the dish will be predominantly monounsaturated; if it is safflower, the result is polyunsaturated.

WHICH OIL?

✧ Safflower and sunflower oils are both light in colour, with a neutral taste, and are interchangeable in recipes. They are ideal for salad dressings, sauteing and baking. Sunflower oil is frequently used in the manufacture of polyunsaturated margarines.

✧ Soya bean oil is light and bland tasting and is the world's leading oil, a major ingredient of blended vegetable oils and polyunsaturated margarines.

OILS AND OILS	
TYPE OF FAT	**OILS**
Polyunsaturated	Safflower, sunflower, walnut, maize (corn), soya bean, wheatgerm, cottonseed, sesame, grapeseed
Monounsaturated	Olive, canola (rapeseed), peanut, avocado
Saturated	Coconut, palm, palm kernel

All oils are mixtures of the three types of fats.
The type occurring in greatest proportion gives the oil its classification.

✧ Peanut oil has a slightly nutty flavour and is preferred in Asian cookery, especially for stir-frying.

✧ Olive oil is enjoying a resurgence in popularity since studies showed that it helps lower blood cholesterol levels. It contains 77% monounsaturated fats, the highest proportion among all vegetable oils, which are thought partly responsible for the lower incidence of heart disease in Mediterranean countries.

✧ Maize or corn oil is derived from the heart of corn kernels and popular in the USA where maize is widely grown. It has a somewhat spicy flavour which develops during cooking, and is predominantly polyunsaturated.

✧ Sesame, walnut, grape seed and avocado are speciality oils which are sold at health food shops and are valued for their exotic flavour.

A few drops of sesame or walnut oil in a salad dressing change its character dramatically and gourmets have long appreciated these expensive oils.

✧ Blended oils are mixtures of several oils. Some are polyunsaturated and this is clearly marked on the label.

✧ Palm and palm kernel oils are derived from an oil palm cultivated in tropical countries. Palm kernel oil, almost 90% saturated, is similar to coconut oil.

✧ Coconut oil is an ingredient in commercial shortenings, biscuits, pies, confectionery and couvertures. It has unique physical characteristics and keeps well without becoming rancid.

GRAPESEED OIL

CALLISTO FRANCESCONI

100% Pure-No

VIRGIN OLIVE OIL
OLAVITA
CAMPOBASSO - ITALY

HEALTHY LIFESTYLES

Cholesterol and heart disease have become intertwined over recent years, yet it must be stressed that high cholesterol is just one of many risk factors influencing the development of heart problems. A healthy lifestyle, in combination with a low fat, low cholesterol diet, can do much towards minimising personal risk.

WEIGHT

Reducing excess weight almost always reduces your blood cholesterol and is a key step in controlling cholesterol.

EXERCISE

Regular moderate exercise is essential for a healthy heart. It can raise the levels of the protective HDL-cholesterol and lower the dangerous LDL-cholesterol. It also has another benefit. It burns up kilojoules (calories) and helps eliminate another serious risk factor – being overweight.

To be beneficial, exercise does not have to be vigorous and sweaty, but it does have to be aerobic. This means any activity that increases the oxygen needs of the body, thus working the heart and lungs. Choose an exercise that you enjoy, that uses the legs, torso or arms, and gets your breathing going; do it for 30 minutes three times a week. Walking, swimming, bicycling, skipping and running are good choices. Start at a modest level and gradually increase your time and intensity. Avoid sudden bursts of fast exercise which can strain an unfit heart.

Weight loss diets are generally low in fat, so what is good for your figure will be good for your heart. Anyone trying to shed weight will find the recipes in this book perfect for both goals.

STRESS

Some Cardiologists designate certain personality types as 'Type A': perfectionist, highly competitive, impatient, always in a hurry and striving to achieve goals. Research has shown that people with marked Type A are especially prone to developing heart disease at an early age. By contrast, 'Type B' people are relaxed and easygoing.

If you recognise tendencies in yourself towards Type A behaviour, start to relearn your 'hurried' way of thinking and give up trying to be a superperson. Learn to say 'no' and to begin to cultivate your spiritual side through activities you find enjoyable.

Long term unrelieved emotional stress is a potential risk factor in many illnesses, not just heart disease. When tension and worries mount up it is important to find ways of 'letting go'. Physical exercise helps lower stress, as does meditation, yoga and Tai Chi.

RISK FACTORS

✧ High blood pressure
✧ High blood cholesterol
✧ Cigarette smoking
✧ Excess weight
✧ Lack of physical activity
✧ Family history (heredity)
✧ Diabetes
✧ Stress

ALCOHOL

A modest intake of alcohol (one or at most two drinks a day) was once considered to confer 'protection' against heart disease. Population studies showed that moderate drinkers suffered fewer heart attacks and lived longer than total abstainers or people who regularly drank more than three drinks daily.

Now, however, new findings reveal that alcohol is detrimental to your heart. A high proportion of abstainers, far from being lifelong teetotallers, were former heavy drinkers who had been forced to give up alcohol because of ill-health such as existing heart trouble, high blood pressure, diabetes and gout. They suffered more heart disease than moderate drinkers, not because they abstained, but because they were a much less healthy group to start with. The message for alcohol now seems clear: less is best.

Pasta

Pasta (spaghetti, macaroni and noodles) is a wonderful food for the heart. It has very little fat, no cholesterol (except for egg noodles) and is high in complex carbohydrates, which makes it a satisfying meal when you're really ravenous. Best of all, it is quick and easy to cook and has endless variations depending on what sauce you serve with it. Remember that cheese, oil or cream in a sauce significantly increase the fat level so try to use lighter sauces based on tomato or vegetables. You'll find more than a little inspiration with our healthy pasta dishes presented here.

❖

GINGERED NOODLES AND VEGETABLES

The flat Oriental noodles that we have used in this recipe are different from egg noodles; they are made from flour and water and are available from Chinese food stores.

Serves 6

- [ ] **1 tablespoon peanut oil**
- [ ] **2 teaspoon grated fresh ginger**
- [ ] **1 clove garlic, crushed**
- [ ] **1 onion, sliced**
- [ ] **1 carrot, sliced diagonally**
- [ ] **2 stalks celery, sliced diagonally**
- [ ] **100 g bean sprouts**
- [ ] **200 g snow peas, trimmed**
- [ ] **500 g flat Oriental noodles, cooked**
- [ ] **freshly ground black pepper**

1   Heat oil in wok or large frypan. Add ginger and garlic, and stir-fry for 1–2 minutes. Stir in onion and carrot, and stir-fry for 4–5 minutes.

2   Add celery, bean sprouts and snow peas, and stir-fry for 2–3 minutes.

3   Stir in noodles, and stir-fry 3–4 minutes or until noodles are heated through. Season to taste with pepper and serve immediately.

---

619 kilojoules (146 calories) per serve		
Fat	3.3 g	low
Cholesterol	0 mg	low
Fibre	3.2 g	high
Sodium	28 mg	low

❖

HERBY TOMATO AND PASTA SALAD

As a luncheon, this salad only needs crusty bread to accompany it.

Serves 6

- [ ] **250 g fresh spinach tagliatelle**
- [ ] **250 g fresh tagliatelle**
- [ ] **2 zucchini, cut into matchsticks**
- [ ] **1 small red capsicum, sliced**
- [ ] **1 small green capsicum, sliced**
- [ ] **200 g green beans, cooked**

TOMATO AND BASIL DRESSING
- [ ] **4 ripe tomatoes, peeled and roughly chopped**
- [ ] **1 clove garlic, crushed**
- [ ] **2 teaspoons olive oil**
- [ ] **2 teaspoons red wine vinegar**
- [ ] **2 tablespoons finely chopped fresh basil**
- [ ] **1 tablespoon finely chopped fresh parsley**
- [ ] **1 tablespoon finely chopped fresh chives**
- [ ] **freshly ground black pepper**

1   Cook both tagliatelles together in boiling water in a large saucepan following packet directions. Rinse under cold running water, drain and set aside to cool completely.

2   Place cold tagliatelles, zucchini, capsicums and beans in a large salad bowl.

3   To make dressing, place tomatoes, garlic, oil and vinegar in a food processor or blender. Process until smooth. Stir in basil, parsley and chives, season to taste with pepper. Spoon dressing over pasta and vegetables. Toss lightly to coat all ingredients with dressing.

622 kilojoules (146 calories) per serve		
Fat	2.1 g	low
Cholesterol	0 mg	low
Fibre	5.0 g	high
Sodium	14 mg	low

Gingered Noodles and Vegetables, Herby Tomato and Pasta Salad, Hot Pasta and Mushrooms

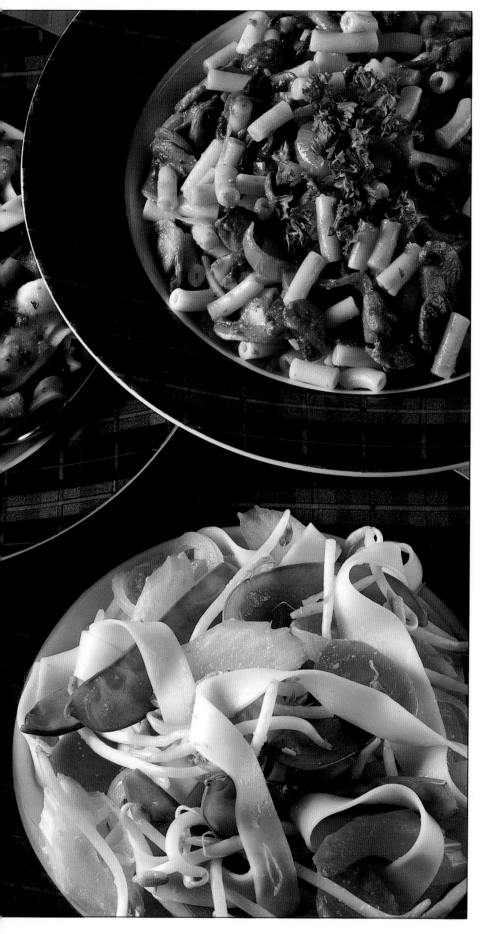

❖

HOT PASTA AND MUSHROOMS

Creamy mushroom sauce and hot pasta – the food that dreams are made of! A green salad and crusty bread will complete your meal.

Serves 4

- ☐ **2 cups (300 g) macaroni**
- ☐ **3 tablespoons finely chopped fresh parsley**
- ☐ **2 tablespoons grated Parmesan cheese**

MUSHROOM SAUCE
- ☐ **2 teaspoons polyunsaturated oil**
- ☐ **1 onion, sliced**
- ☐ **500 g mushrooms, sliced**
- ☐ **1 teaspoon paprika**
- ☐ **2 tablespoons tomato paste (no added salt)**
- ☐ **1 cup (250 mL) evaporated skim milk**
- ☐ **freshly ground black pepper**

1   Cook macaroni in boiling water in a large saucepan following packet directions. Drain, set aside and keep warm.

2   To make sauce, heat oil in a non-stick frypan. Cook onion and mushrooms until they soften. Blend together paprika, tomato paste and milk. Stir into mushroom mixture and cook gently over low heat for 5 minutes. Season to taste with pepper.

3   Place pasta in a heated serving dish and spoon over sauce. Toss gently to combine. Sprinkle with parsley and Parmesan to serve.

945 kilojoules (223 calories) per serve

Fat	*3.9 g*	*low*
Cholesterol	*7 mg*	*low*
Fibre	*4.4 g*	*med*
Sodium	*155 mg*	*med*

RAVIOLI WITH TUNA SAUCE

Serves 4

- ☐ **375 g fresh or frozen ravioli with spinach filling**
- ☐ **2 tablespoons grated Parmesan cheese**
- ☐ **fresh dill sprigs**

TUNA SAUCE
- ☐ **2 teaspoons olive oil**
- ☐ **1 onion, finely chopped**
- ☐ **1 clove garlic, crushed**
- ☐ **440 g canned tomatoes (no added salt), undrained and mashed**
- ☐ **1 tablespoon tomato paste (no added salt)**
- ☐ **1 tablespoon dry red wine**
- ☐ **1 teaspoon sugar**
- ☐ **425 g canned tuna in spring water, drained and flaked**
- ☐ **1 tablespoon finely chopped fresh parsley**
- ☐ **1 tablespoon finely chopped fresh dill**
- ☐ **freshly ground black pepper**

1   Cook ravioli in boiling water in a large saucepan following packet directions. Drain and keep warm.

2   To make sauce, heat oil in a frypan. Cook onion and garlic for 4–5 minutes or until onion softens. Stir in tomatoes, tomato paste, wine and sugar. Bring to the boil. Add tuna, parsley and dill, reduce heat and simmer for 10 minutes.

3   Place pasta on a warmed serving platter. Spoon over sauce, sprinkle with Parmesan cheese and garnish with dill sprigs.

1187 kilojoules (283 calories) per serve

Fat	16.0 g	high
Cholesterol	40 mg	low
Fibre	2.5 g	med
Sodium	165 mg	med

SPAGHETTI WITH ASPARAGUS SAUCE

Serves 6

- ☐ **500 g spaghetti**
- ☐ **2 tablespoons grated Parmesan cheese**

ASPARAGUS SAUCE
- ☐ **500 g fresh asparagus spears, trimmed**
- ☐ **1 tablespoon olive oil**
- ☐ **1 thick slice wholegrain bread, crumbed**
- ☐ **1 cup (250 mL) evaporated skim milk**
- ☐ **60 g grated mozzarella cheese**
- ☐ **freshly ground black pepper**

1   Cook spaghetti in boiling water in a large saucepan following packet directions.
2   To make sauce, steam, boil or microwave asparagus until tender. Drain and refresh under cold running water. Cut into 3 cm pieces and set aside. Heat oil in a frypan, add breadcrumbs and cook over low heat for 2 minutes, stirring all the time. Stir in milk and asparagus, and cook over medium heat for 5 minutes. Mix in cheese and continue to cook until melted. Season to taste with pepper.
3   Place spaghetti on a warmed serving platter, spoon over sauce and toss gently to combine. Sprinkle with Parmesan cheese and serve immediately.

1000 kilojoules (237 calories) per serve

Fat	6.7 g	med
Cholesterol	11 mg	low
Fibre	2.4 g	med
Sodium	188 mg	med

TASTY TOMATO AND MACARONI BAKE

Serves 6

- ☐ **2 cups (300 g) wholemeal macaroni**
- ☐ **2 teaspoons grape seed oil**
- ☐ **2 large onions, sliced**
- ☐ **1 red capsicum, sliced**
- ☐ **1 green capsicum, sliced**
- ☐ **1/2 cup (125 mL) tomato paste (no added salt)**
- ☐ **2 large tomatoes, peeled and sliced**
- ☐ **2 tablespoons finely chopped fresh basil**
- ☐ **3 cups (750 mL) Cheese Sauce (see page 17)**

TOPPING
- ☐ **2 teaspoons olive oil**
- ☐ **1 tablespoon finely chopped fresh chives**
- ☐ **3 tablespoons grated mozzarella cheese**
- ☐ **1 tablespoon grated Parmesan cheese**

1 Cook macaroni in a large saucepan of boiling water following packet directions. Drain, rinse under cold running water and spread over the base of a 16 cm x 28 cm shallow ovenproof dish.

2 Heat oil in a non-stick frypan. Cook onions and red and green capsicums for 5 minutes or until they soften. Drain off any liquid and mix in tomato paste.

3 Spread over macaroni, top with tomato slices, sprinkle with basil and spoon over cheese sauce.

4 To make topping, mix together oil, chives, mozzarella and Parmesan cheeses. Sprinkle on top of macaroni mixture and bake at 180°C for 20 minutes or until topping is golden and macaroni bake is heated through.

811 kilojoules (192 calories) per serve

Fat	5.0 g	low
Cholesterol	7 mg	low
Fibre	3.7 g	high
Sodium	10 mg	low

Quark

Quark or quarg is a continental-style cottage cheese which is packed in a solid mass and is not separate curd particles usually seen in cottage cheese. It has a sharper, more acidic taste, making it less popular for sweet dishes and more suitable for savoury ones.

Quark is usually made from skim milk and so has a very low fat content of around 1 per cent – ideal for a healthy heart diet. Be sure to check the label before buying, as it can also be made from full cream milk which gives it a high fat content. The label will give an indication of this as 'full cream quark'. It is generally packaged in a soft plastic envelope or a sausage-shaped pack and is available through many delicatessens or specialty shops. A 20 gram serving has 63 kilojoules or 15 calories.

Ricotta

(see Cheese)

Ricotta is a soft unriped curd cheese. It is similar in food value to cottage cheese, but its fat content can be higher if whole milk or cream is added, so check the label if you are uncertain. Ricotta makes an excellent substitute for cream, cream cheese and sour cream.

Top left: Spaghetti with Asparagus Sauce, Ravioli with Tuna Sauce
Bottom left: Tasty Tomato and Macaroni Bake

Shellfish

Shellfish are frequently avoided by people trying to lower cholesterol as they have heard that shellfish are high in cholesterol. Readings are not as high as was once thought, because earlier analyses measured a number of sterols as well as cholesterol, giving a false high reading. Apart from prawns, all shellfish contain low to moderate amounts and can be safely included in your meals. Recent Australian tests show that shellfish are extremely low in fat and what little fat they carry is high in the unique omega-3 fats which can improve our blood profile and immune system.

❖

FRUITY SEASIDE SLAW

Serves 4

- ☐ **20 scallops**
- ☐ **4 cooked large prawns, peeled and deveined**
- ☐ **1/4 red cabbage, shredded**
- ☐ **250 g seedless green grapes**
- ☐ **400 g canned mango slices, drained and liquid reserved**
- ☐ **3 tablespoons low fat unflavoured yoghurt**
- ☐ **1 tablespoon chopped fresh chives**
- ☐ **1 tablespoon chopped fresh dill**
- ☐ **1 teaspoon grated fresh ginger**
- ☐ **1/4 teaspoon curry powder**
- ☐ **pinch chilli powder**

1   Poach scallops in water for 3–4 minutes. Drain and set aside to cool.
2   Combine scallops, prawns, cabbage, grapes and mango slices in a salad bowl.
3   Blend together yoghurt, 2 tablespoons of reserved mango liquid, chives, dill, ginger, curry and chilli powders. Fold lightly through salad. Refrigerate until required.

994 kilojoules (234 calories) per serve

Fat	1.9 g	low
Cholesterol	81 mg	med
Fibre	6.0 g	high
Sodium	301 mg	high

❖

SEAFOOD PAELLA

Serves 6

- ☐ **1 1/2 tablespoons olive oil**
- ☐ **2 spanish onions, finely chopped**
- ☐ **4 cloves garlic, crushed**
- ☐ **1 green capsicum, thinly sliced**
- ☐ **1 red capsicum, thinly sliced**
- ☐ **1 tablespoon finely chopped fresh tarragon**
- ☐ **1/4 teaspoon ground turmeric**
- ☐ **2 cups (500 mL) chicken stock**
- ☐ **3 tomatoes, peeled and chopped**
- ☐ **1 tablespoon tomato paste (no added salt)**
- ☐ **1/2 cup (125 mL) dry white wine**
- ☐ **3 tablespoons lemon juice**
- ☐ **2 cups (420 g) quick cooking brown rice**
- ☐ **200g fresh or frozen peas**
- ☐ **4 white fish fillets, cut into pieces**
- ☐ **18 shelled oysters**
- ☐ **150 g scallops**
- ☐ **18 mussels in shells, cleaned**
- ☐ **freshly ground black pepper**

1   Heat oil in a large heavy-based frypan. Cook onions, garlic, capsicums and tarragon for 3–4 minutes.
2   Combine turmeric, stock, tomatoes, tomato paste, wine and lemon juice. Add to pan with rice. Cover and simmer for 12 minutes.

CHOLESTEROL IN SHELLFISH	
Milligrams per 100 g uncooked shellfish, shell and bone removed	
Scallops	29
Oysters	40
Mussels	45
Crab	68
Lobster	98
Octopus	140
Cuttlefish	160
Squid (calamari)	160
Prawns	170–190
Average	140

Fish Marketing Authority 1989, except for oysters, scallops and mussels from CSIRO Food Research Quarterly 37 (1977), 33–39.

3   Remove cover and stir in peas, fish, oysters, scallops and mussels. Season to taste with pepper. Simmer for a further 15 minutes or until rice is tender. Discard any unopened mussels before serving.

1389 kilojoules (332 calories) per serve

Fat	7.9 g	med
Cholesterol	105 mg	high
Fibre	5.0 g	high
Sodium	396 mg	high

❖

SCALLOP AND PRAWN STICKS

Add an exotic touch to your next barbecue with these easy to prepare and tasty kebabs.

Serves 6

- ☐ **6 uncooked king prawns, shelled and deveined**
- ☐ **500 g scallops**
- ☐ **1 large onion, cut into eighths**

MARINADE
- ☐ **1 tablespoon olive oil**
- ☐ **2 tablespoons white wine**
- ☐ **2 teaspoons finely chopped fresh dill**
- ☐ **2 teaspoons finely chopped fresh parsley**
- ☐ **2 teaspoons finely chopped fresh chives**
- ☐ **2 cloves garlic, crushed**
- ☐ **2 teaspoons grated lime rind**
- ☐ **2 tablespoons lime juice**
- ☐ **freshly ground black pepper**

1   Thread prawns, scallops and onions onto six wooden skewers.
2   To make marinade, combine oil, wine, dill, parsley, chives, garlic, lime rind and juice in a glass dish. Season to taste with pepper. Add skewered seafood and marinate for 1 hour.
3   Remove seafood from marinade and grill for 2–3 minutes each side, turning and brushing with marinade frequently.

650 kilojoules (154 calories) per serve

Fat	4.4 g	low
Cholesterol	93 mg	med
Fibre	0.8 g	low
Sodium	350 mg	high

Fruity Seaside Slaw, Seafood Paella, Scallop and Prawn Sticks

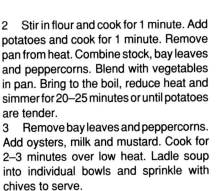

OYSTER CHOWDER

Serves 4

- [ ] **20 g polyunsaturated margarine (salt reduced)**
- [ ] **1 onion, chopped**
- [ ] **1 stalk celery, sliced**
- [ ] **1 carrot, diced**
- [ ] **2 tablespoons plain flour**
- [ ] **2 potatoes, peeled and diced**
- [ ] **3 cups (750 mL) chicken stock**
- [ ] **2 bay leaves**
- [ ] **6 peppercorns**
- [ ] **16 shelled oysters**
- [ ] **$^1/_2$ cup (125 mL) evaporated skim milk**
- [ ] **1 teaspoon Dijon-style mustard**
- [ ] **2 tablespoons chopped fresh chives**

1   Melt margarine in a large heavy-based saucepan. Cook onion, celery and carrot for 3–4 minutes or until tender.

2   Stir in flour and cook for 1 minute. Add potatoes and cook for 1 minute. Remove pan from heat. Combine stock, bay leaves and peppercorns. Blend with vegetables in pan. Bring to the boil, reduce heat and simmer for 20–25 minutes or until potatoes are tender.

3   Remove bay leaves and peppercorns. Add oysters, milk and mustard. Cook for 2–3 minutes over low heat. Ladle soup into individual bowls and sprinkle with chives to serve.

801 kilojoules (156 calories) per serve

Fat	*4.8 g*	*low*
Cholesterol	*21 mg*	*low*
Fibre	*3.4 g*	*high*
Sodium	*318 mg*	*high*

DID YOU KNOW?

There is a pearl of truth in the belief that oysters are an aphrodisiac food. Oysters are the richest food source of zinc, an essential mineral needed for sexual maturation in adolescence and for sperm production in adult males. Unfortunately no one has yet discovered how many you need to eat to improve your love life!

PASTA MUSSELS AND WINE SAUCE

Serves 4

- [ ] **250 g wholemeal spaghetti**
- [ ] **2 cloves garlic, crushed**
- [ ] **2 onions, chopped**
- [ ] **1 cup (250 mL) dry white wine**
- [ ] **$^1/_2$ cup (125 mL) water**
- [ ] **1 sprig fresh thyme**
- [ ] **2 tablespoons chopped fresh parsley**
- [ ] **1 kg mussels, cleaned and bearded**
- [ ] **fresh thyme sprigs**
- [ ] **fine strips lemon peel**

SAUCE

- [ ] **20 g polyunsaturated margarine (salt reduced)**
- [ ] **2 tablespoons plain flour**
- [ ] **$^1/_2$ cup (125 mL) evaporated skim milk**
- [ ] **1 tablespoon lemon juice**
- [ ] **freshly ground black pepper**

1   Cook pasta in a large saucepan of boiling water, following packet directions. Drain and keep warm.

2   Place garlic, onions, wine, water, thyme and parsley in a large saucepan. Bring to the boil and cook for 5 minutes. Drop in mussels, reduce heat and simmer for 5 minutes.

3   Remove mussels from pan with a slotted spoon. Discard any unopened shells. Set remaining mussels aside and keep warm. Strain cooking liquid and reserve.

4   To make sauce, melt margarine in a small saucepan. Stir in flour and cook for 1–2 minutes. Remove from heat and gradually blend in reserved cooking liquid. Cook over medium heat until sauce boils and thickens.

5   Whisk in milk and lemon juice. Season to taste with pepper and heat through gently. Place pasta on a warm serving platter, top with mussels and spoon over sauce. Garnish with shallots and lemon peel.

1386 kilojoules (326 calories) per serve

Fat	*7.1 g*	*med*
Cholesterol	*126 mg*	*med*
Fibre	*2.0 g*	*med*
Sodium	*356 mg*	*high*

Pasta Mussels and Wine Sauce, Oyster Chowder

CHOLESTEROL CHECKLIST

Our handy fact finder will sort out the confusion surrounding cholesterol today.

LDL-CHOLESTEROL

Low Density Lipoprotein-Cholesterol. One of the two major forms of cholesterol circulating in the blood. It accounts for most of the cholesterol and contributes to the fatty build-up on artery walls, which encourages heart disease.

HDL-CHOLESTEROL

High Density Lipoprotein - Cholesterol. The second major form of blood cholesterol and the 'good guy', which clears cholesterol from the arteries and protects against heart disease. Athletes and people from long-lived families usually have high levels of this cholesterol. When you have your cholesterol measured, you will receive one figure for the total, plus another set of figures for the two cholesterol forms separately or as a ratio.

LIPIDS

A medical term meaning fats.

TRIGLYCERIDES

Another important type of fat found in food and in the body. Like blood cholesterol, a high reading (over 2 millimoles per litre) increases the likelihood of heart disease, but is not considered as dangerous a risk factor as high blood cholesterol.

OMEGA - 3 FATS

Unique polyunsaturated fats found in fatty fish, which have the ability to reduce blood clotting and to lessen its 'stickiness'. They can lower blood pressure and triglyceride levels (but not cholesterol), and so help protect against heart disease. May also help fight immune-related problems such as asthma, rheumatoid arthritis, and the skin complaint psoriasis.

CONVERTING CHOLESTEROL

Blood cholesterol can be measured in millimoles per litre (mmol/l) or in milligrams per decilitre (mg/dl or mg%). Here is a handy conversion table for both measurements. In Australia, the National Heart Foundation recommends that your cholesterol be under 5.5 mmol/l.

mg/dL	mmol/L
180	4.66
185	4.78
190	4.91
195	5.04
200	5.17
205	5.30
210	5.43
215	5.56
220	5.69
225	5.82
230	5.95
235	6.08
240	6.21
245	6.34
250	6.47
255	6.60
260	6.72
265	6.85
270	6.98
275	7.11
280	7.24
285	7.37
290	7.50
295	7.63
300	7.76

FISH OIL

A thick, oily liquid extracted from fish flesh, not fish livers. It is a concentrated form of fish, with 2–3 grams of fish oil being equivalent to eating 200 grams of an oily fish. It supplies a high dose of omega-3 fats. Because of its unpleasant taste, it is more popular in capsule form which is tasteless.

EPA

Eicosapentaenoic acid – one of the most common Omega-3 fats. It is a polyunsaturated fat, which remains liquid at very low temperatures, keeping the fish mobile in extreme cold. Found in all fish and shell fish, but especially rich in oily fish such as herring, salmon, tuna, mackerel, sardines, and ocean trout.

P:S RATIO

The ratio of polyunsaturated to saturated fats in a food. Often appearing on the labels of margarines, mayonnaises and oils, a P:S ratio of 2:1 means that there is twice as much polyunsaturated fat present as saturated.

HYDROGENATED FAT

A fat or oil which has been made more solid by the addition of hydrogen to the fat's molecule. Hydrogenation is an important step in the manufacture of margarine, as it allows the use of a range of oils depending on their availability.

Teas

Tea, whether hot or cold, weak or strong, is a wonderfully refreshing drink. If drunk black, without milk or sugar, it has no kilojoules (calories). Herbal teas such as peppermint, rosehip, chamomile and fenugreek are increasing in popularity and make an interesting variation on regular tea. Some contain no caffeine or theophylline, the stimulant compounds of tea and coffee, and this is usually listed on the pack.

Tea has many uses apart from just a drink. It can be an ingredient in dishes as diverse as cakes and chutney and, as our tea recipes show, adds its own unique flavour.

❖

ICED TEA

Icy cool tea served with lemon slices makes the ideal thirst quencher for midsummer.

Serves 4

- ☐ **4 tea bags**
- ☐ **4 cups (1 litre) cold water**
- ☐ **ice cubes**
- ☐ **lemon slices**

1   Place water and tea bags in a large glass jug. Cover and refrigerate overnight.
2   To serve, place ice cubes in long glass, pour in tea and garnish with lemon slices.

5 kilojoules (1 calories) per serve

Fat	0 g	low
Cholesterol	0 mg	low
Fibre	0 g	low
Sodium	0 mg	low

COOK'S TIP

Using cold water to make iced tea ensures that your tea will be a clear amber and prevents an acid taste. Using hot water and allowing the tea to cool tends to give a cloudy liquid with a bitter taste.

❖

BERRY-FILLED TEA PANCAKES

In these pancakes we replaced milk with tea for a more robust flavour. We have filled our pancakes with a creamy berry fruit filling but you might like to serve them warm with honey and lemon juice, or with a savoury filling of your choice.

Makes 10

PANCAKES
☐ **100 g plain flour, sifted**
☐ **1 egg, lightly beaten**
☐ **1 cup (250 mL) cold tea**
☐ **1 tablespoon polyunsaturated oil**
☐ **2 tablespoons icing sugar, sifted**

FILLING
☐ **1 cup (250 g) ricotta cheese**
☐ **1 cup (250 g) low fat unflavoured yoghurt**
☐ **2 tablespoons rosewater**
☐ **100 g fresh strawberries, hulled and halved**
☐ **100 g raspberries**
☐ **2 kiwi fruit, sliced**

1   To make pancakes, place flour in a bowl and make a well in the centre. Add egg and work flour in from the sides. Stir in tea a little at a time to make a smooth batter of pouring consistency. Set aside to stand for 30 minutes before cooking.
2   Pour 2 tablespoons batter into a lightly greased non-stick frypan. Cook pancakes until golden brown each side.
3   To make filling, place ricotta, yoghurt and rosewater in food processor or blender. Process until smooth. Transfer to a bowl and fold through fruit. To serve, divide filling between pancakes. Roll up and dust with icing sugar.

559 kilojoules (133 calories) per serve

Fat	5.0 g	low
Cholesterol	31 mg	low
Fibre	1.8 g	med
Sodium	75 mg	low

❖

HOT GINGER TEA

Iced tea in summer, hot ginger tea in winter. It is a particularly comforting drink for a cold.

Serves 4

☐ **3 teaspoons black tea leaves**
☐ **1/2 teaspoon grated fresh ginger**
☐ **4 cups (1 L) boiling water**
☐ **lemon juice (optional)**
☐ **honey (optional)**

1   Place tea and ginger in a warmed teapot. Pour over boiling water, stir and allow to steep for 5 minutes. Stir again and strain before pouring.
2   Flavour tea with lemon juice and honey if desired.

88 kilojoules (20 calories) per serve

Fat	0 g	low
Cholesterol	0 mg	low
Fibre	0 g	low
Sodium	0 mg	low

Hot Ginger Tea, Iced Tea, Berry-Filled Tea Pancakes

Tofu
(Soya Bean Curd)

Tofu, a white soya bean curd, makes a wonderful low fat, cholesterol free substitute for cream, mayonnaise and cheese in cooking. With its bland flavour, it can lend itself to either savoury or sweet dishes, as our recipes illustrate. Although it has been an important food in China and Japan for over two centuries, the West is only now discovering the delights of this ancient food.

❖

SESAME CHICKEN STIR-FRY

Serves 6

- ☐ **250 g tofu, drained, pressed and cubed**
- ☐ **300 g chicken fillets, cut into strips**
- ☐ **2 teaspoons polyunsaturated oil**
- ☐ **2 teaspoons sesame oil**
- ☐ **1 teaspoon grated ginger**
- ☐ **$^1/_2$ red capsicum, sliced**
- ☐ **$^1/_2$ green capsicum, sliced**
- ☐ **2 teaspoons cornflour blended with $^1/_2$ cup (125 mL) water**
- ☐ **4 shallots, sliced diagonally**
- ☐ **1 cup (50 g) bean sprouts**
- ☐ **1 tablespoon sesame seeds, toasted**

MARINADE
- ☐ **2 tablespoons low salt soy sauce**
- ☐ **1 tablespoon dry sherry**
- ☐ **1 clove garlic, crushed**

1   To make marinade, mix together soy sauce, sherry and garlic. Add tofu and chicken, toss to coat and leave to marinate for 30 minutes. Drain and reserve marinade.
2   Heat oils in a wok or frypan and cook tofu, chicken and ginger for 5 minutes or until chicken is just cooked. Remove tofu and chicken, set aside and keep warm.
3   Toss in red and green capsicums and cook for 3–4 minutes. Return tofu and chicken to pan. Toss to combine. Mix cornflour mixture with reserved marinade. Stir into pan and cook until mixture boils and thickens. Toss in shallots, bean sprouts and sesame seeds. Serve immediately.

576 kilojoules (139 calories) per serve		
Fat	7.0 g	med
Cholesterol	34 mg	low
Fibre	0.7 g	low
Sodium	229 mg	med

FAT FIGHTER
Tofu has less than 5% fat, no cholesterol and virtually no sodium (salt). Being extracted from soya beans, it is a good source of protein, minerals and B vitamins. One-third of a cup of tofu (75 g) supplies only 200 kilojoules (48 calories).

❖

FRUITY TOFU SAUCE

Makes 2 cups (500 mL)

- ☐ **250 g tofu, drained and roughly chopped**
- ☐ **250 g strawberries, hulled and roughly chopped**
- ☐ **2 tablespoons honey**

1   Place tofu, strawberries and honey in a food processor or blender and process until smooth.
2   Cover and chill. Stir well before serving.

60 kilojoules (14 calories) per serve		
Fat	0.3 g	low
Cholesterol	0 mg	low
Fibre	0.2 g	low
Sodium	2 mg	low

Left: Fruity Tofu Sauce
Below: Sesame Chicken Stir-Fry, Curried Vegetable and Tofu Soup

❖

CURRIED VEGETABLE AND TOFU SOUP

Serves 6

- ☐ 1 tablespoon polyunsaturated oil
- ☐ 1 large onion, chopped
- ☐ 1 clove garlic, crushed
- ☐ 1 teaspoon ground cumin
- ☐ 1 teaspoon ground coriander
- ☐ 1 teaspoon ground turmeric
- ☐ 1/2 teaspoon chilli powder
- ☐ 1/2 small cauliflower, cut into small florets
- ☐ 1 carrot, diced
- ☐ 1 large potato, diced
- ☐ 1 zucchini, sliced
- ☐ 4 cups (1 litre) vegetable stock
- ☐ 250 g tofu, drained, pressed and cut into cubes
- ☐ 320 g canned corn kernels (no added salt)
- ☐ freshly ground black pepper
- ☐ 3 tablespoons chopped fresh dill

1   Heat oil in a large saucepan and cook onion, garlic, cumin, coriander, turmeric and chilli powder for 4–5 minutes. Stir in cauliflower, carrot, potato, zucchini and stock. Bring to the boil. Reduce heat, cover and simmer for 15–20 minutes or until vegetables are tender.

2   Using a slotted spoon remove 1 cup of cooked vegetables and puree in a food processor or blender.

3   Stir puree, tofu and corn into soup and heat gently for a further 4–5 minutes. Season to taste with pepper. Sprinkle with dill to serve.

768 kilojoules (184 calories) per serve

Fat	5.0 g	low
Cholesterol	0 mg	low
Fibre	6.1 g	high
Sodium	91 mg	low

Unrefined Foods

Unrefined foods, sometimes called 'wholefoods', were once the province of health food freaks and vegetarians, but are now very much recommended for their fibre content. Brown rice, wholemeal pastas, lentils, dried beans, grains such as oats, barley and buckwheat are all unrefined foods that are kind to not only to your heart but to your whole body.

Vegetables

There are so many reasons why vegetables are vital to your diet. They add crunch, colour and vitality to your food. They have no cholesterol or fat (except for avocados and olives); they are packed with vitamins, minerals and fibre; they are so low in kilojoules (calories) that you can eat them quite freely; and the type of fibre they contain helps lower cholesterol.

❖

BEETROOT, ORANGE AND HORSERADISH SALAD

Serves 6

- ☐ **4 medium cooked beetroot, peeled and cut into thin strips**
- ☐ **2 teaspoons grated orange rind**
- ☐ **2 oranges, segmented**

HORSERADISH DRESSING
- ☐ **1¹/₂ tablespoons olive oil**
- ☐ **3 tablespoons cider vinegar**
- ☐ **1 teaspoon mustard powder**
- ☐ **2 teaspoons horseradish relish**
- ☐ **2 teaspoons sugar**

1   Combine beetroot, orange rind and orange segments. Arrange attractively in a salad bowl. Cover and refrigerate for 1–2 hours.

2   To make dressing, combine oil, vinegar, mustard, horseradish and sugar in a screwtop jar. Shake well to combine. Pour over salad just prior to serving.

260 kilojoules (62 calories) per serve

Fat	0.5 g	low
Cholesterol	0 mg	low
Fibre	3.5 g	high
Sodium	50 mg	low

❖

CANDIED KUMERA

Serve this sweet vegetable with grilled pork chops.

Serves 6

- ☐ **¹/₂ cup (85 g) brown sugar**
- ☐ **¹/₂ cup (125 mL) water**
- ☐ **20 g polyunsaturated margarine (salt reduced)**
- ☐ **500 g kumera, peeled and thinly sliced**
- ☐ **2 tablespoons toasted slivered almonds**

1   Combine brown sugar, water and margarine in a non-stick frypan. Cook over low heat until margarine melts. Add kumera, cover and continue to cook over low heat for 15–20 minutes or until kumera is tender.

2   Add almonds and toss lightly to combine.

636 kilojoules (151 calories) per serve

Fat	4.4 g	low
Cholesterol	0 mg	low
Fibre	2.3 g	med
Sodium	32 mg	low

STIR-FRIED BROCCOLI WITH ALMONDS

A colourful stir-fry that is sure to please the whole family.

Serves 4

- [ ] **2 carrots, cut into matchsticks**
- [ ] **500 g broccoli, cut into florets**
- [ ] **2 teaspoons peanut oil**
- [ ] **1 onion, sliced**
- [ ] **1 clove garlic, crushed**
- [ ] **2 teaspoons grated fresh ginger**
- [ ] **2 teaspoons low salt soy sauce**
- [ ] **2 tablespoons toasted almonds**

1 Boil, steam or microwave carrots and broccoli until they just change colour. Drain and refresh under cold running water.

2 Heat oil in wok or frypan. Add onion, garlic and ginger and stir-fry for 4–5 minutes. Add carrots, broccoli and soy sauce, and stir-fry for 3–4 minutes longer, or until vegetables are heated through. Just prior to serving toss through almonds.

390 kilojoules (92 calories) per serve

Fat	4.9 g	low
Cholesterol	0 mg	low
Fibre	7.6 g	high
Sodium	86 mg	low

Beetroot, Orange and Horseradish Salad, Candied Kumera, Stir-Fried Broccoli with Almonds

APPLE, STRAWBERRY AND PECAN SALAD

A variation on the traditional Waldorf salad, with half the fat and no cholesterol.

Serves 4

- ☐ **2 red apples, chopped**
- ☐ **2 stalks celery, sliced**
- ☐ **200 g strawberries, halved**
- ☐ **3 tablespoons sultanas**
- ☐ **60 g chopped pecans**

DRESSING
- ☐ **2 teaspoons finely chopped fresh mint leaves**
- ☐ **3 tablespoons low fat unflavoured yoghurt**
- ☐ **2 tablespoons lemon juice**

1   Combine apples, celery, strawberries, sultanas and pecans in a bowl.
2   To make dressing, blend together mint, yoghurt and lemon juice. Toss with apple mixture and refrigerate until required.

739 kilojoules (176 calories) per serve

Fat	7.9 g	med
Cholesterol	0 mg	low
Fibre	5.0 g	high
Sodium	43 mg	low

POTATO AND BRUSSELS SPROUTS SOUP

Serves 4

- ☐ **250 g Brussels sprouts, trimmed**
- ☐ **2 large potatoes, peeled and diced**
- ☐ **4 cups (1 L) chicken stock**
- ☐ **1/2 cup (125 mL) skim milk**
- ☐ **freshly ground black pepper**
- ☐ **2 tablespoons chopped walnuts**

1   Place sprouts, potatoes and stock in a saucepan and bring to the boil. Reduce heat, cover and simmer for 20–25 minutes or until potatoes are tender. Remove from heat and set aside to cool slightly.
2   Place in a food processor or blender and puree. Return soup to a clean pan, add milk and season to taste with pepper. Heat gently. To serve, ladle into soup bowls and sprinkle with walnuts.

524 kilojoules (126 calories) per serve

Fat	4.3 g	low
Cholesterol	0 mg	low
Fibre	3.2 g	high
Sodium	41 mg	low

THE TOP TEN FOR FIBRE

Grams of fibre per average serve of vegetables

Broccoli, 2/3 cup	3.9
Sweetcorn, 1/2 cup kernels	3.5
Potato, unpeeled 1	3.0
Carrot, peeled, 1	2.9
Eggplant, 1/2	2.7
Pumpkin, peeled, 1/2 cup	2.4
Tomato, raw, 1	2.4
Potato, peeled, 1	2.4
Onion, 1	2.2
Cauliflower, 2/3 cup	2.0
All figures refer to cooked vegetables, except tomato which is raw	

*Left: Apple, Strawberry and Pecan Salad
Below: Potato and Brussel Sprouts Soup, Minestrone Soup*

MINESTRONE SOUP

Minestrone is a substantial main meal soup, both tasty and filling. You can vary the vegetables depending on what is available.

Serves 8

- [ ] **2 tablespoons olive oil**
- [ ] **3 cloves garlic, crushed**
- [ ] **1 onion, chopped**
- [ ] **1 large potato, diced**
- [ ] **1 carrot, diced**
- [ ] **2 large zucchini, diced**
- [ ] **100 g green beans, trimmed and sliced**
- [ ] **2 tablespoons finely chopped fresh parsley**
- [ ] **1 tablespoon finely chopped fresh basil**
- [ ] **1 teaspoon finely chopped fresh oregano**
- [ ] **3 tablespoons tomato paste (no added salt)**
- [ ] **6 cups (1.5 litres) chicken stock**
- [ ] **freshly ground black pepper**
- [ ] **440 g canned red kidney beans, drained**
- [ ] **100 g macaroni noodles**
- [ ] **1/2 cabbage, finely shredded**

1   Heat oil in a large heavy-based saucepan. Cook garlic and onion for 2–3 minutes. Stir in potato, carrot, zucchini and beans. Cook for 3–4 minutes, stirring frequently.

2   Combine parsley, basil, oregano, tomato paste and stock. Pour over vegetables in pan. Season to taste with pepper. Cover and simmer for 30 minutes or until vegetables are tender.

3   Add undrained kidney beans. Bring to the boil, drop in macaroni and cook for a further 20 minutes. Add cabbage during last minute of cooking.

753 kilojoules (180 calories) per serve		
Fat	4.6 g	low
Cholesterol	0 mg	low
Fibre	4.0 g	high
Sodium	111 mg	low

TOMATO AND SPINACH STUFFED MUSHROOMS

Serves 6

- ☐ **6 large flat mushrooms**
- ☐ **3 tablespoons grated mozzarella cheese**
- ☐ **1 tablespoon grated Parmesan cheese**
- ☐ **1 tablespoon chopped fresh chives**

FILLING
- ☐ **1 tablespoon olive oil**
- ☐ **1 clove garlic, crushed**
- ☐ **3 shallots, finely chopped**
- ☐ **2 spinach leaves, stalk removed and finely shredded**
- ☐ **1 tablespoon tomato paste (no added salt)**
- ☐ **³/₄ cup (45 g) fresh breadcrumbs**
- ☐ **freshly ground black pepper**

1   Wipe mushrooms, remove stalks and finely chop.
2   To make filling, heat 1 teaspoon oil in frypan, cook garlic and shallots for 1–2 minutes. Stir in spinach and tomato paste, cook for 2–3 minutes. Fold through breadcrumbs. Season to taste with pepper.
3   Brush mushroom caps with remaining oil and place on an oven tray. Combine mozzarella and Parmesan cheeses. Spoon filling into mushroom caps, top with cheese mixture and sprinkle with chives. Bake at 200°C for 10–15 minutes.

371 kilojoules (89 calories) per serve

Fat	4.8 g	low
Cholesterol	6 mg	low
Fibre	1.6 g	med
Sodium	106 mg	low

❖

GIPSY BAKED POTATOES

Serves 4

- ☐ **2 teaspoons polyunsaturated oil**
- ☐ **1 onion, chopped**
- ☐ **1 clove garlic, crushed**
- ☐ **1 teaspoon finely chopped fresh rosemary**
- ☐ **3 large tomatoes, peeled and chopped**
- ☐ **1 green capsicum, diced**
- ☐ **1 teaspoon paprika**
- ☐ **1 cup (250 mL) chicken stock**
- ☐ **freshly ground black pepper**
- ☐ **2 large potatoes, peeled and cut into thick slices**
- ☐ **2 tablespoons finely chopped fresh chives**

1   Heat oil in a frypan and cook onion, garlic and rosemary for 4–5 minutes or until onion softens. Add tomatoes, capsicum, paprika and chicken stock, bring to the boil and simmer for 10 minutes. Season to taste with pepper.
2   Arrange potatoes in layers in a lightly greased ovenproof dish and spoon over tomato sauce. Bake at 180°C for 1¹/₂ hours or until cooked through. Sprinkle with chives just prior to serving.

538 kilojoules (129 calories) per serve

Fat	2.3 g	low
Cholesterol	0 mg	low
Fibre	5.6 g	high
Sodium	108 mg	low

❖

HERBY VEGETABLE SALAD

Serves 4

- ☐ **¹/₄ cauliflower, broken into florets**
- ☐ **1 head broccoli, broken into florets**
- ☐ **1 large carrot, cut into thin strips**
- ☐ **150 g snow peas, trimmed**
- ☐ **1 red capsicum, cut into thin strips**
- ☐ **3 tablespoons lemon juice**
- ☐ **2 teaspoons finely chopped fresh coriander**
- ☐ **2 teaspoons finely chopped fresh rosemary**
- ☐ **freshly ground black pepper**

LEMON VINAIGRETTE
- ☐ **2 tablespoons lemon juice**
- ☐ **1 tablespoon olive oil**
- ☐ **1 clove garlic, crushed**
- ☐ **1 teaspoon wholegrain mustard**

1   Boil, steam or microwave cauliflower, broccoli, carrot and snow peas until just tender. Drain, refresh under cold water.
2   Drain vegetables well. Toss in a salad bowl with capsicum, lemon juice, coriander and rosemary. Season to taste with pepper. Refrigerate until required.
3   To make vinaigrette, combine all ingredients in a screwtop jar. Shake well to combine. Pour over salad just prior to serving.

348 kilojoules (82 calories) per serve

Fat	4.5 g	low
Cholesterol	0 mg	low
Fibre	5.0 g	high
Sodium	38 mg	low

Tomato and Spinach Stuffed Mushrooms, Herby Vegetable Salad, Gipsy Baked Potatoes

Lettuce Roll-ups, French Bean Salad

3   Blend together vinegar and olive oil, pour over beans and refrigerate for 1–2 hours. Sprinkle with sesame seeds and serve.

276 kilojoules (66 calories) per serve

Fat	5.1 g	med
Cholesterol	0 mg	low
Fibre	3.8 g	high
Sodium	5 mg	low

NUTRITION TIP

✧ Frozen vegetables, picked and processed at their peak, retain most of their nutritional value. If cooked when frozen, they will have around the same food value as home-cooked fresh ones.

✧ When compared by weight, the vegetable which is lowest in kilojoules (calories) is celery, then cucumber and lettuce. Three long sticks of celery, 20 lettuce leaves or $^1/_2$ cucumber contain the same kilojoules as half a slice of bread.

LETTUCE ROLL-UPS

An interesting side dish or light entree, these roll-ups can be prepared several hours in advance.

Serves 6

☐ **6 large lettuce leaves**
☐ **1 cup (60 g) bean sprouts**
☐ **2 mangoes, peeled and chopped**
☐ **260 g canned sliced water chestnuts, drained**
☐ **2 teaspoons finely chopped preserved ginger**
☐ **2 teaspoons finely chopped mint leaves**
☐ **3 tablespoons low fat mayonnaise**
☐ **1 tablespoon low fat unflavoured yoghurt**

1   Tear lettuce leaves in half lengthways. Toss together sprouts, mangoes, water chestnuts, ginger and mint.
2   Combine mayonnaise and yoghurt. Fold through mango mixture.
3   Place a spoonful of mixture on each lettuce leaf. Roll up tightly and secure with a toothpick.

581 kilojoules (141 calories) per serve

Fat	3.5 g	low
Cholesterol	3 mg	low
Fibre	4.3 g	high
Sodium	80 mg	low

FRENCH BEAN SALAD

Serves 4

☐ **500 g green beans, trimmed and sliced**
☐ **1 clove garlic, crushed**
☐ **1 teaspoon ground fenugreek**
☐ **2 tablespoons finely chopped fresh mint leaves**
☐ **1 teaspoon red wine vinegar**
☐ **1 tablespoon olive oil**
☐ **2 teaspoons toasted sesame seeds**

1   Boil, steam or microwave beans until just tender. Drain and place in a salad bowl.
2   Combine garlic, fenugreek and mint. Toss with warm beans. Set aside and allow to cool slightly.

Water

Water is a most wonderful drink. It has no kilojoules, no fat, caffeine or sugar. Icy cold or with a squeeze of lemon or lime, it makes an ideal thirst quencher in hot weather. More and more restaurants are offering water to refresh and cleanse the palate; scores of 'water purifiers' have appeared to meet the desire for cleaner tasting water.

Nutritionists recommend that you drink six to eight glasses of fluid a day, especially if you are in a humid or air-conditioned environment. Try and drink at least half of these in the form of healthy water.

Yoghurt
and Buttermilk

Yoghurt and buttermilk are two cultured dairy products, their tangy slightly acidic flavour being produced by the action of bacteria on milk. Cultured or soured dairy foods are traditional in many parts of the world. They are known to be easier to digest than fresh milk, probably because they contain little lactose (milk sugar), which causes digestive problems for two-thirds of the world's people.

Low fat yoghurt is the best choice for people trying to lower cholesterol and has many culinary uses. It is an excellent substitute for cream, sour cream and mayonnaise and can be used in both savoury and sweet dishes (sweetened fruit yoghurt is the most popular form).

Buttermilk has the same food value as skim milk and makes a refreshing drink in summer. It too is a useful low fat ingredient and you can learn to cook with it by following our delicious recipes.

❖

SPICY CURRY DIP

Yoghurt is the ideal base for many dips. When a recipe calls for sour cream replace it with yoghurt to allow those watching their cholesterol to indulge as well. Serve this dip with vegetables such as blanched asparagus spears, raw carrot and celery sticks and cherry tomatoes.

Makes 1 cup (250 mL)

- ☐ **2 teaspoons polyunsaturated oil**
- ☐ **1 small onion, chopped**
- ☐ **1 teaspoon curry powder**
- ☐ **pinch chilli powder**
- ☐ **1 cup (250 mL) low fat yoghurt**
- ☐ **freshly ground black pepper**

1   Heat oil in a non-stick frypan and cook onion with curry and chilli powders for 4–5 minutes or until onion softens.

2   Whisk into yoghurt and season to taste with pepper. Chill until ready to serve.

77 kilojoules (18 calories) per serve

Fat	0.9 g	low
Cholesterol	2 mg	low
Fibre	0 g	low
Sodium	19 mg	low

❖

BEEF SALAD STROGANOFF

Make this wonderful summer salad from leftover roast beef. For an attractive presentation you might like to serve the salad in lettuce cups garnished with sprigs of coriander.

Serves 6

- ☐ **1 tablespoon polyunsaturated margarine (salt reduced)**
- ☐ **200 g button mushrooms, sliced**
- ☐ **1 tablespoon lemon juice**
- ☐ **500 g lean roast beef, cut into strips**
- ☐ **6 shallots, finely chopped**
- ☐ **2 tablespoons chopped fresh coriander**
- ☐ **1 cup (250 g) low fat unflavoured yoghurt**
- ☐ **freshly ground black pepper**

1   Heat margarine in a non-stick frypan and cook mushrooms with lemon juice for 4–5 minutes. Drain and set aside to cool.
2   Combine mushrooms, beef, shallots and coriander. Add yoghurt and toss lightly to combine. Season to taste with pepper.

761 kilojoules (183 calories) per serve

Fat	7.3 g	med
Cholesterol	58 mg	low
Fibre	1.2 g	low
Sodium	107 mg	low

Beef Salad Stroganoff, Spicy Curry Dip

CREAMY LEMON AND LIME PIE

A light chiffon-style pie that's sure to become an entertaining favourite.

Serves 8

BASE
- [ ] **1 quantity sweet bran pastry (pg 9)**

FILLING
- [ ] **2 tablespoons gelatine dissolved in 4 tablespoons boiling water**
- [ ] **1 cup (250 mL) evaporated skim milk, chilled**
- [ ] **2 tablespoons fresh lime juice**
- [ ] **2 tablespoons fresh lemon juice**
- [ ] **1 teaspoon grated lime rind**
- [ ] **1 cup (250 mL) low fat unflavoured yoghurt**
- [ ] **3 egg whites**
- [ ] **$^1/_2$ cup (125 g) caster sugar**
- [ ] **250 g mixed berries**

1   To make base, roll pastry to a 25 cm circle. Bake on a lightly greased oven tray at 200°C for 30–35 minutes or until cooked through. Remove from oven and using the base of a 20 cm springform pan as guide, cut to fit the pan. Allow to cool completely.
2 To make filling, set gelatine mixture aside to cool. Beat evaporated milk until thick. Blend together lime juice, lemon juice, lime rind and yoghurt. Fold through evaporated milk and gelatine mixture.
3   Beat egg whites until soft peaks form, then continue beating while slowly adding sugar until stiff peaks form. Fold egg white mixture through milk mixture. Place pastry base in a 20 cm springform pan. Top with filling and chill until set. Just before serving top pie with berries.

864 kilojoules (204 calories) per serve

Fat	*4.7 g*	*low*
Cholesterol	*3 mg*	*low*
Fibre	*1.9 g*	*med*
Sodium	*75 mg*	*low*

COOL 'N' FRUITY

Yoghurt ice blocks make wonderful summer coolers for the cholesterol conscious. They can be made in any flavours you like; our three favourites are banana, strawberry and pineapple. To make six yoghurt ice blocks you will require 1 cup of mashed or pureed fresh fruit and 1 cup of low fat unflavoured yoghurt. Combine and mix well. Spoon into ice block containers or small plastic cups and freeze. If making banana ice blocks, mix 1 teaspoon of lemon juice into the mashed banana to prevent discolouring.

CHOCOLATE CAKE

Surprise your cholesterol watchers with this chocolate cake.

Serves 16

- [ ] **1 $^1/_2$ cups (180 g) self-raising flour**
- [ ] **1 tablespoon cocoa**
- [ ] **$^3/_4$ cup (190 g) sugar**
- [ ] **1 tablespoon golden syrup**
- [ ] **100 g polyunsaturated margarine, melted**
- [ ] **$^1/_2$ cup (125 mL) buttermilk, warmed**
- [ ] **$^1/_2$ cup (125 mL) skim milk, warmed**

ICING
- [ ] **60 g reduced fat spread (salt reduced), softened**
- [ ] **3-4 tablespoons skim milk**
- [ ] **3 cups icing sugar**
- [ ] **2 tablespoons cocoa**

1   Sift together flour and cocoa into a bowl. Add sugar. Combine golden syrup, margarine, buttermilk and skim milk. Stir into dry ingredients and mix well to combine.
2   Spoon cake into a lightly greased and lined 18 cm round cake pan. Bake at 180°C for 30 minutes. Remove and allow to cool.
3   To make icing, combine spread and milk. Mix in icing sugar and cocoa. Beat for 5 minutes or until mixture is lightly and fluffy. Ice cold cake.

1625 kilojoules (374 calories) per serve

Fat	*9.2 g*	*med*
Cholesterol	*0 mg*	*low*
Fibre	*0 g*	*low*
Sodium	*322 mg*	*high*

QUICK WHOLEMEAL AND FRUIT ROLLS

Serves 8

- [ ] **2 cups (270 g) wholemeal flour**
- [ ] **2 cups (250 g) self-raising flour**
- [ ] **$^1/_2$ teaspoon ground nutmeg**
- [ ] **$^1/_2$ teaspoon ground cinnamon**
- [ ] **1 cup (160 g) dried mixed fruit**
- [ ] **1 $^1/_2$ cups (375 mL) buttermilk**

1   Sift together wholemeal and self-raising flours, nutmeg and cinnamon. Mix in dried fruit.

2   Stir in buttermilk a little at a time and beat until dough is firm and leaves the sides of the bowl.

3   Turn out on a lightly floured board and knead briefly. Divide into eight portions and shape into rolls. Place on a lightly greased oven tray. Bake at 200°C for 30-35 minutes or until well risen and golden.

1108 kilojoules (260 calories) per serve		
Fat	2.2 g	low
Cholesterol	0 mg	low
Fibre	5.5 g	high
Sodium	619 mg	high

YOGHURT INSTEAD

❖   If a recipe calls for buttermilk and you do not have any, you can use yoghurt in its place. You will, however, need to thin the yoghurt to about the same consistency as buttermilk. Use $^1/_2$ cup (125 mL) yoghurt to 1 cup (250 mL) water or skim milk.

❖   Yoghurt can also be used to replace sour cream in a recipe. The dish will have a slightly tangier flavour when yoghurt is used. For sweet dishes, add a teaspoon of sugar for each cup of yoghurt if you wish.

Above: Chocolate Cake, Quick Wholemeal and Fruit Rolls
Left: Creamy Lemon and Lime Pie

Zucchini

Zucchini or courgettes are in fact baby marrows. This wonderful vegetable can be eaten cooked or raw. Why don't you try making a zucchini salad using a combination of sliced yellow and green zucchini tossed in our Minty Lemon dressing (page 18). This salad looks particularly pretty if the zucchini is sliced diagonally.

USEFUL INFORMATION

In this book, ingredients such as fish and meat are given in grams so you know how much to buy. A small inexpensive set of kitchen scales is always h ndy and very easy to use. Other ingredients in our recipes are given in tablespoons and cups, so you will need a nest of measuring cups (1 cup, $^1/2$ cup, $^1/3$ cup and $^1/4$ cup), a set of spoons (1 tablespoon, 1 teaspoon, $^1/2$ teaspoon and $^1/4$ teaspoon) and a transparent graduated measuring jug (1 litre or 250 mL) for measuring liquids. Cup and spoon measures are level.

MEASURING UP

Metric Measuring Cups

$^1/4$ cup	60 mL	2 fl.oz
$^1/3$ cup	80 mL	2$^1/2$ fl.oz
$^1/2$ cup	125 mL	4 fl.oz
1 cup	250 mL	8 fl.oz

Metric Measuring Spoons

$^1/4$ teaspoon	1.25 mL
$^1/2$ teaspoon	2.5 mL
1 teaspoon	5 mL
1 tablespoon	20 mL

MEASURING LIQUIDS

Metric	Imperial	Cup
30 mL	1 fl.oz	
60 mL	2 fl.oz	$^1/4$ cup
90 mL	3 fl.oz	
125 mL	4 fl.oz	$^1/2$ cup
170 mL	5 $^1/2$ fl.oz	$^2/3$ cup
185 mL	6 fl.oz	
220 mL	7 fl.oz	
250 mL	8 fl.oz	1 cup
500 mL	16 fl.oz	2 cups
600 mL	1 pint	

MEASURING DRY INGREDIENTS

Metric	Imperial
15 g	$^1/2$ oz
30 g	1 oz
60 g	2 oz
90 g	3 oz
125 g	4 oz
155 g	5 oz
185 g	6 oz
220 g	7 oz
250 g	8 oz
280 g	9 oz
315 g	10 oz
350 g	11 oz
375 g	12 oz
410 g	13 oz
440 g	14 oz
470 g	15 oz
500 g	16 oz (1 lb)
750 g	1 lb 8 oz
1 kg	2 lb
1.5 kg	3 lb
2 kg	4 lb
2.5 kg	5 lb

QUICK CONVERTER

Metric	Imperial
5 mm	$^1/4$ in
1 cm	$^1/2$ in
2 cm	$^3/4$ in
2.5 cm	1 in
5 cm	2 ins
10 cm	4 ins
15 cm	6 ins
20 cm	8 ins
23 cm	9 ins
25 cm	10 ins
30 cm	12 ins

OVEN TEMPERATURES

°C	°F	Gas Mark
120	250	$^1/2$
140	275	1
150	300	2
160	325	3
180	350	4
190	375	5
200	400	6
220	425	7
240	475	8
250	500	9

GLOSSARY OF TERMS

TERM	MEANING
Baste	To moisten meat or vegetables during cooking
Beetroot	Regular round beet
Bicarbonate of soda	Baking soda
Bottled oysters	Oysters preserved in brine, if unavailable use bottled mussels
Breadcrumbs, fresh	1 or 2 day old bread made into crumbs
Breadcrumbs, packaged	Use commercially packaged breadcrumbs
Butterfly pork steaks	Double pork loin steaks
Butternut pumpkin	Butternut squash
Evaporated skim milk	If unavailable use low fat evaporated milk
Capsicum	Red or green bell peppers
Chilli sauce	A sauce which includes chillies, salt and vinegar
Cholesterol free mayonnaise	A mayonnaise made from polyunsaturated oil without egg yolks
Cornflour	Cornstarch, substitute arrowroot
Ginger	Fresh ginger is ginger root. Preserved ginger is root ginger cooked in syrup
Glace ginger	Crystallised ginger
Golden nugget pumpkin	A summer squash, if unavailable use acorn squash
Grape seed oil	A polyunsaturated oil made from grape seeds, if unavailable use any polyunsaturated oil such as sunflower or safflower oil
King prawns	Scampi or Dublin Bay prawns
Kumera	Orange coloured sweet potato
Lebanese cucumber	Ridge cucumber
Muffin pans	Deep tartlet pans, if unavailable line tartlet pans with paper cake cases
Polyunsaturated oil	A vegetable oil high in polyunsaturated fats such as corn, soya or sunflower
Rice bran	If unavailable substitute oat bran
Shallots	Spring onions
Snow peas	Mangetout
Sour cream	Commercially soured cream
Tomato paste	Tomato puree
White vinegar	Distilled malt vinegar
Yellow lentils	Yellow dhal available from Indian shops
Zucchini	Courgettes

BIG FAT SECRETS

HANDY FAT CHECKLIST

Check the amount of fat contained in 100 grams of each food.

(Expressed as grams per 100 grams or per cent).

Oil	100
Lard, dripping	100
Margarine, butter	80
Mayonnaise, rich	78
Desiccated coconut	63
Bacon	59
Tartare sauce	54
Peanuts, roasted	47
Salami	45
Puff pastry	36
Cream	36
Sour cream	35
Potato chips	33
Cheddar cheese	33
Milk chocolate	31
Corn chips	27
Shortbread biscuits	26
Chocolate eclair	26
Sesame bar	26
Cream-filled biscuits	25
Carob and nut bar	25
Croissant	24
Camembert cheese	24
Avocado	23
Cheesecake	22
Doughnut	20
Sausage roll	20
Beef, lamb, pork, fatty	20–25

INDEX

ACKNOWLEDGEMENTS
The publishers would like to thank The National Heart Foundation of Australia for their assistance during the production.

Admiral Appliances; Black & Decker (Australasia) Pty Ltd; Blanco Appliances; Knebel Kitchens; Leigh Mardon Pty Ltd; Master Foods of Australia; Meadow Lea Foods; Namco Cookware; Ricegrowers' Co-op Mills Ltd; Sunbeam Corporation Ltd; Tycraft Pty Ltd distributors of Braun, Australia; White Wings Foods for their assistance during recipe testing.

Accoutrement, Australia East India Company, China Doll, Classic Ceramics, Country Floors, Dansab, Decor Gifts, Ikea, Inini, Lifestyle Imports, Limoges, Made in Japan, Noritake, Royal Doulton, The Bay Tree, Wedgwood for their assistance during photography.

The Committee of Direction of Fruit Marketing, for supplying Avocado photograph.